Декабрь 2020

Даниил,

С рождеством !

Может быть , мы приедем
сюда однажды. Холодно!

С любовью,

Кристабель   x

Sophie Panzer
Christina Simmel

GAZPROM CITY
ГАЗПРОМ СИТИ

SCHLEBRÜGGE.EDITOR

Zwischen Nowy Urengoi und UKPG-16 I
Между Новым Уренгоем и УКПГ-16 I
Between Novy Urengoy and UKPG-16 I

66° 33′ 44″ N

●	Nowy Urengoi | Новый Уренгой | Novy Urengoy
1	Moskau | Москва | Moscow
2	Archangelsk | Архангельск | Arkhangelsk
3	Murmansk | Мурманск
4	Workuta | Воркута | Vorkuta
5	Norilsk | Норильск
6	Jakutsk | Якутск | Yakutsk
7	Magadan | Магадан
8	Anchorage | Анкоридж
9	Yellowknife | Йеллоунайф
10	Nuuk | Нуук
11	Reykjavík | Рейкьявик
12	Tromsø | Тромсё

—————— 10 °C Juli Isotherm | 10 °C Июль Изотерма | 10 °C July Isotherm
·············· Permafrostzone | Зона вечной мерзлоты | Permafrost zone

Anfang Februar fliegen wir mit der russischen S7 Airlines von Moskau nach Nowy Urengoi – Russlands Erdgashauptstadt in Westsibirien. Der Flug ist bis auf den letzten Platz ausgebucht. Kaum ein älterer Passagier ist an Bord und die jüngeren sind definitiv nicht für eine Polarexpedition ausgerüstet. Nur wir schwitzen in dicken Daunenjacken und Winterstiefeln. Fast dreieinhalb Stunden dauert der Flug, fast ebenso lange überfliegen wir eine schier endlose Schneewüste. Hin und wieder taucht in der Morgendämmerung eine kleine Siedlung oder der Schein einer Gasfackel auf.

Ohne Gulnas Kolokolowa, eine freundliche Mitarbeiterin von Gazprom, und ohne den Schranken öffnenden *Propusk*, jenen Passierschein, der uns als Gäste des Erdgasförderunternehmens ausweist, wäre unsere Reise an der Passkontrolle zu Ende gewesen. Die Stadt ist für Ausländer gesperrt. Um sie zu besuchen, benötigt man eine Sondergenehmigung des Energiekonzerns. Zahllose Anfragen haben wir an Gazprom gerichtet, unermüdlich haben wir nachgehakt und nachgefragt, bis es aus der Zentrale in Moskau endlich grünes Licht gab.

Woher rührt das Interesse, an den nördlichen Polarkreis zu reisen, in diese Stadt, die weniger mit Sehenswürdigkeiten als mit großer Industrie aufwarten kann und wo das Klima meist rau und frostig ist?

Die wechselseitige Abhängigkeit von Europa und Russland durch Erdgasimporte und -exporte und die gewichtige Position von Gazprom wird regelmäßig in Politik und Medien thematisiert. Welche Konsequenzen diese Abhängigkeit für die Konsumenten am europäischen Ende der Erdgasleitung hat, steht dabei meist im Vordergrund. Die Voraussetzungen der Förderung und die daran geknüpften Lebensbedingungen für die Menschen an der Quelle in Westsibirien werden hingegen weniger oft diskutiert.

Wie leben die Menschen in Nowy Urengoi, in einer Großstadt, die vollkommen von der Ressource Erdgas abhängig und in der das Leben ganz und gar im Konzern-Rhythmus getaktet ist?

Vor dem Flughafen auf dem Parkplatz zeigt eine digitale Anzeige minus 45 Grad Celsius. Die Brille vereist binnen Sekunden, das Atmen tut weh. Wir werden bereits von einem Fahrer von Gazprom erwartet und in das Hotel „Polarstern" gebracht. In den kommenden zehn Tagen wollen wir die Konzernstadt kennenlernen und so viel Alltag wie möglich miterleben.

Jenseits der Großen Erde
STIMMEN AUS EINER STADT AM POLARKREIS

„Die Stadt Nowy Urengoi gibt es nur, weil es hier das Urengoi-Gasfeld gibt. Ohne dieses Rohstoffvorkommen gäbe es die Stadt nicht. Man nennt unsere Stadt auch ‚Erdgashauptstadt' oder einfach Gazprom City."

Beinahe 50 Jahre ist es her, dass in Westsibirien das Gasfeld Urengoi, eines der größten zusammenhängenden Gasfelder der Erde, entdeckt wurde. Weit entfernt von besiedeltem Gebiet, in der sumpfigen Seenlandschaft der subarktischen Tundra, wurde mit dem systematischen Aufbau der Erdgasindustrie begonnen.

Viele Freiwillige zogen in diese unwirtliche Gegend, in der von September bis Mai die Temperaturen unter dem Gefrierpunkt liegen und das Quecksilber nicht selten auf minus 50 Grad sinkt, um an diesem ambitionierten Vorhaben mitzuwirken. Transportwege wurden gebaut, Förderanlagen errichtet, hunderte Kilometer von Pipelines verlegt und Schritt für Schritt wuchs aus einer kleinen Ansiedlung für die Arbeiter die nördliche Großstadt Nowy Urengoi.

Eduard Kondratjew ist acht Jahre alt, als seine Eltern Mitte der 1970er Jahre mit ihren drei Kindern aus dem Süden Russlands an den Polarkreis ziehen, um hier, wie Tausende andere, beim Aufbau der Erdgasindustrie anzupacken und Geld zu verdienen.

„Ich erinnere noch genau, wie damals alles war. Es sind ganz besondere Eindrücke, die mich wohl mein ganzes Leben begleiten, sie sind so stark, dass ich wahrscheinlich ihretwegen niemals von hier weggehe. Das macht der besondere Geist des Nordens! In den ersten Jahren lebten wir in sogenannten ‚Fässern', ähnlich aufgebockten Waggons. Meist lebten zwei oder sogar drei Familien zusammen auf vielleicht 15 Quadratmetern. Die Eltern fuhren morgens zur Arbeit und die Kinder blieben zurück, mit selbst gebasteltem Spielzeug aus Konservendosen. Das sind wahrlich nachhaltige Erlebnisse."

Ein knapp elf Kilometer langer, schmaler Streifen, am südlichen Ende des Urengoi-Gasfeldes, begrenzt durch zwei Zuflüsse des Pur und umringt von abertausend Seen und Tümpeln, die im Winter unter einer dicken Schneedecke verschwinden, wurde als Ort für die Stadt der Erdgasarbeiter bestimmt, eine Tafel mit dem Ortsnamen symbolisch neben die temporären Herbergen der Arbeiter in den Boden gerammt. Eduard war dabei, als die kärglichen Unterkünfte und die Holzhütten der ersten Siedler stattlichen Wohnmodulen wichen, als Straßenzüge und Wohnviertel angelegt und Leitungen in den Permafrostboden gehauen wurden, um die Bewohner komfortabel mit Licht und Wärme zu versorgen.

Der Aufbau der Stadt war schnell nach den Regeln der sozialistischen Stadtplanung auf dem Reißbrett skizziert. Entlang der Magistrale wurden standardisierte Wohneinheiten hochgezogen, gruppiert um einen Innenhof mit einem öffentlichen Gebäude, meist einer Schule oder einem Kindergarten. Das Baukombinat Nr. 3 aus Leningrad lieferte die vorgefertigten Betonelemente für die Wohnhäuser, den Plattenbautyp 1-LG-600. Die 600er Serie wird auch einfach „das Schiff" genannt, denn die langen horizontalen Fensterbänder erinnern an einen Ozean-Liner.

Ein Bau gleicht dem anderen, nur die bunten Fassaden bieten Orientierungshilfe. Mehrere Wohnblöcke bilden die einzelnen Wohnviertel, die sogenannten Mikrorajons. Sie tragen klingende Namen und sind den „Optimisten" und „Enthusiasten" gewidmet, sowie den „Erbauern der Straßen" – oder auch einfach bloß der „Polarlandschaft" und dem „Sonnenschein". Zwischen den Wohnvierteln liegen das Krankenhaus, die Verwaltungsgebäude und Freizeiteinrichtungen. Ein eindeutiges Stadtzentrum gibt es nicht. Als Wohnraum knapp wurde, breitete sich die Stadt jenseits des Flusses aus. Der nördliche Teil Sewerka mit den Wohnvierteln „Freundschaft", „Frieden", „Sowjet" und „Jubiläum" wurde angelegt.

Mittlerweile ist Nowy Urengoi eine wohlhabende Metropole mit mehr als 110.000 Einwohnern, und gut drei Viertel des russischen Erdgases wird in einem komplexen System von Förderanlagen rund um die Stadt produziert – aufgebaut und kontrolliert von dem heutigen Konzern Gazprom. Die Mehrzahl der Einwohner ist in der Erdgasbranche tätig, bei Gazprom oder bei einer der unzähligen Tochter- und Partnerfirmen.

Auch der 44-jährige Eduard kann auf eine Karriere bei Gazprom zurückblicken. Viele unterschiedliche Aufgaben hat er im Laufe der Jahre übernommen. Heute ist er leitender Ingenieur bei Gazprom Dobycha Jamburg. Lockende Angebote aus der Gazprom-Zentrale in Moskau, in der Hauptstadt zu arbeiten, hat es durchaus gegeben. Doch aus Leidenschaft für den Norden ist er in Nowy Urengoi geblieben. Hier hat er seine Frau Lena kennengelernt und seine Kinder Jurij, Alexandra und Katja großgezogen. In seiner Freizeit genießt er, was die Natur zu bieten hat – sei es das Entdecken von Rentieren, Schneehühnern und weißen Polarfüchsen, die er nicht jagt, sondern beobachtet und fotografiert, sei es das Fischen in einem der glasklaren Flüsse der westsibirischen Tundra.

„Man muss nur aus dem Fenster schauen, um zu sehen, was hier Wunderbares passiert. Alles ist groß – die Natur, der Raum und die Weite sind unfassbar. Die Produktion und die Technologie sind riesig. Es gibt so viele Schätze, die im Boden verborgen sind. Hier ist auch die Arbeit grenzenlos."

Viele, meist junge Russen, zieht es heute noch in den Norden, um in der Konzernstadt gutes Geld zu verdienen. Ein Job in der Erdgasbranche steht für ein gesichertes und für russische Verhältnisse hohes Einkommen. Sie nehmen ein Leben in einer der abgeschiedensten Gegenden der Erde, ganz und gar bestimmt von der Rohstoffindustrie, in Kauf.

„Als Nowy Urengoi gegründet wurde, gab es hier einen stadtformenden Betrieb, den heutigen Konzern Gazprom, der die wesentliche Infrastruktur, also Straßen, Kindergärten, Schulen und Wohnhäuser, errichtet hat. Heute liegt diese Verantwortung in unseren Händen."

Gemeint sind die Hände von Jewgeni Woroschilow, des hauptverantwortlichen Stadtplaners von Nowy Urengoi. Vor drei Jahren ist der auf der Krim geborene Architekt mit Frau und zwei Kindern an den Polarkreis gezogen, um diesen Posten zu übernehmen. Seit dem Jahr 2006 obliegen die Stadtentwicklung und die Kontrolle über sämtliche Bauvorhaben dem Amt für Stadtplanung, bis dahin gehörten diese Tätigkeiten zum Aufgabenbereich von Gazprom.

Nowy Urengoi funktioniere, so die Einschätzung des Architekten, im Großen und Ganzen wie jede andere Stadt auch, sie liege eben nur am Polarkreis. Es gibt ein Kraftwerk, eine Müllverbrennungs- und eine Kläranlage. Lebensmittel werden größtenteils angeliefert, teilweise aber auch selbst produziert. Es gibt eine Brot- und Fleischwarenfabrik und ein großes Gewächshaus. Frische Milch wird in der Erdgashauptstadt nicht mehr produziert – aus

Kostengründen wurden die Kühe aus dem Norden umgesiedelt. In der Freizeit geht man ins Kino, ins Erdgas-Museum oder zum Bowling in die „Polareule", zu einer Vorstellung in den Kulturpalast oder in eine der gigantischen Sporthallen. Es gibt eine orthodoxe Kirche und eine Moschee. Menschen verschiedenster Nationalitäten haben sich zu Zeiten der Sowjetunion in der Stadt niedergelassen: Russen, Weißrussen, Ukrainer, Tataren, Kumyken, Aserbaidschaner, Baschkiren oder Tschetschenen.

„Nowy Urengoi ist eine Stadt für die Erdgasarbeiter. Sie wurde von Freiwilligen mit großem Ehrgeiz erbaut. Viele haben an der Errichtung mitgeholfen, haben etwas beigetragen, sich angefreundet. Hier gibt es diesen besonderen Geist, der die harten Bedingungen erträglich macht. Es ist eine funktionale Stadt, in der die Architektur dem Nutzen untergeordnet ist. Die ganze Stadt ist ein Denkmal der Arbeit und derer, die sie errichtet und die die Erdgasfelder erschlossen haben."

Seit der Erschließung des Urengoi-Gasfeldes wurden 6,5 Billionen Kubikmeter Gas gewonnen – Spitzenleistung und Eintrag in das Guinness-Buch der Rekorde! Noch nie wurde solch eine gigantische Menge Erdgas aus einer einzigen Lagerstätte gefördert – und das Urengoi-Gasfeld sollte nicht die einzige Lagerstätte bleiben, die in diesem Erdgas-Eldorado entdeckt und erschlossen wurde: Das Jamburg-Gasfeld wurde 1986 angezapft, Sapoljarnoje im Jahr 2001, Juschno-Russkoje und Beregowoje gingen 2007 ans Netz, Samburgskoje 2012. Eine derartige Erfolgsgeschichte wird freilich nicht nur in Statistiken festgehalten oder in Pressemeldungen veröffentlicht.

Gazprom, russischer Recke!
Planet Gazprom
Vorwärts, Gazprom! Vorwärts Gazprom!

So die Titel der Hymnen, die den weltweit größten Energiekonzern und seine Erfolgsgeschichte in Wort und Ton verherrlichen und an patriotische Arbeiterlieder vergangener Sowjetzeiten erinnern.

Gazprom, bis 1992 dem Ministerium für Erdöl und Gaswirtschaft unterstellt, ist seitdem eine Aktiengesellschaft. Der Staat besitzt 50 Prozent und eine Aktie und hat im Aufsichtsrat die Mehrheit der Sitze. Mit seinen rund 459.000 Beschäftigten ist Gazprom einer der größten Arbeitgeber des Landes und unterstützt den russischen Staatshaushalt mit Milliardenüberweisungen, ist wichtigster Devisenlieferant des Landes und bedeutendster Energieversorger für viele Länder Mitteleuropas, die auf den Rohstoff aus Westsibirien angewiesen sind.

Durch die Erschließung immer weiter entfernt liegender Gasfelder hat Nowy Urengoi die Funktion eines Brückenkopfes: Die Stadt gewährleistet das Anlanden der Erdgasarbeiter, die von dort zu ihren Arbeitsplätzen weiterreisen. Zeitweilig arbeiten über 20.000 Schichtarbeiter auf den Gasfeldern rund um Nowy Urengoi. Viele pendeln aus entfernten Gegenden Russlands, andere direkt aus der Erdgashauptstadt. Gazprom Dobycha Jamburg und Gazprom Dobycha Urengoi haben ihre Firmenzentralen in der Stadt. Von hier aus steuern sie die Förderung und den Transport des Rohstoffes innerhalb Russlands und weiter ins Ausland und koordinieren die Heerscharen von Angestellten, die für die Erdgasgewinnung unverzichtbar sind.

Vom Flughafen verlassen Busse mit Arbeitern die Stadt Richtung Sapoljarnoje. Das Erdgasfeld liegt 220 Kilometer nordöstlich von Nowy Urengoi. An der Stadtgrenze gibt es Straßenposten. In diesem strategisch wichtigen Gebiet wird nicht nur der Besucher aus dem Ausland kontrolliert, sondern jeder, der sich von A nach B bewegen möchte. Fällt die Außentemperatur unter minus 45 Grad, müssen die Busse aus Sicherheitsgründen in Kolonne fahren. Die Trasse ist gut ausgebaut, die Landschaft tief verschneit. Man erahnt den Fluss Pur, der durch die Tiefebene mäandert. An den Ufern stehen Birken, Lärchen, Zirbelkiefern und Fichten. Nach kurzer Fahrtzeit dann ein vollkommen anderes Bild: eine weiße, grenzenlose Schneewüste. Der Blick wird durch nichts festgehalten, weder durch Hügel oder Wälder noch durch Ortschaften, und endet erst am Horizont. Abwechslung in diese monotone Landschaft bringen nur die stählernen, vereisten Überlandmasten und vereinzelte Gasfackeln – das Signum von Gazprom.

Bei diesen hohen Minusgraden und bei bestimmtem Sonneneinfall verwandeln kerzengerade, bunte Lichtsäulen die Schneewüste endgültig in eine surreale Kulisse. Sehr real dagegen sind die vielen Laster, Busse und Geländewagen, die über die eisige Trasse fahren. Dass hier in der kurzen schneefreien Zeit, im Juni, Juli und August, Pflanzen gedeihen, die Tundra blüht, Pilze aus dem Boden schießen, die verschiedensten Beeren Blüten treiben und wenig später Früchte tragen, ist jetzt unvorstellbar, aber wahr. Der Sommer dauert gerade einmal 35 Tage.

Inmitten dieses grenzenlosen Schneefeldes, 60 Kilometer nördlich des Polarkreises, steht UKPG-2S, eine der fünf Gasaufbereitungsanlagen von Sapoljarnoje. Nur nach einer erneuten Ausweiskontrolle darf man das eingezäunte Betriebsgelände betreten. Der Industriekomplex besteht aus mehreren Hallen und einem kilometerlangen Leitungssystem. Rund um die Gasaufbereitungsanlage strömt das Erdgas aus bis zu 3.000 Metern Tiefe an die Erdoberfläche und gelangt über aufgebockte Röhren in eine fast menschenleere Fabrikshalle. Man hört keine Stimmen, nur das monotone Rauschen und Pfeifen der Maschinen. Ein Gewirr von großen und kleinen farbigen Leitungen, Turbinen, Tanks und Messapparaturen, die Menge, Dichte, Druck und Temperatur prüfen. Nicht Schweiß und Schmiere, sondern Hightech auf allerhöchstem Niveau!

„Wir fördern hier 130 Milliarden Kubikmeter Gas im Jahr. Das ist mehr als der jährliche Gasverbrauch in Deutschland. Das Gas ist hochwertig, es besteht zu 99,8 Prozent aus Methan. Die Rückstände Propan, Butan und Stickstoff sind minimal. Und Wasser haben wir auch nicht viel, nur 200 Gramm auf tausend Kubikmeter geförderten Gases."

Asad Gumerow, der stellvertretende Leiter dieser Anlage, arbeitet schon seit Jahren auf den westsibirischen Gasfeldern. Nicht ohne Stolz berichtet er von der außerordentlichen Förderleistung, die hier erbracht wird, Zahlen und Daten hat er sofort parat.

Nur selten sieht man auf dem Gelände einen Techniker mit weißem Helm und blauer Jacke mit dem Gazprom-Logo. Vorbei sind die Zeiten, als Ende des vergangenen Jahrhunderts der moorige Tundraboden mit meterhohem Sand aufgeschüttet wurde, vorbei die Zeiten, als riesige Bohrköpfe in die Gasflöze vorgedrungen sind und Geröll und Schlamm an die Erdoberfläche ausgeworfen haben. Heute ist UKPG-2S ein fast klinisch sauberer Betrieb. Alle Vorgänge werden per Computer gesteuert. Tag und Nacht verfolgen zwei Dispatcher an großen Bildschirmen die einzelnen Schritte der Gasaufbereitung. Die Daten werden an das „Herz", wie das Kontrollzentrum genannt wird, weitergegeben. Die Mitarbeiter hier tragen keine Gazprom-Kluft, sondern einen dunklen Anzug. Treten irgendwo in diesem hochkomplizierten Netzwerk Unregelmäßigkeiten auf, warnen rote Lämpchen. Ein Bildschirm zeigt an, wie viel Gas in den letzten zwei Stunden gefördert wurde und vergleicht die Menge mit dem täglichen Soll. Die Stimmung ist entspannt. Mit einem Auge verfolgen die jungen Männer ein Eishockeyspiel im Fernsehen.

Bevor das Gas die Anlage verlässt, wird aus sicherheitstechnischen Gründen ein Duftstoff beigemengt, da Erdgas von Natur aus farb- und geruchlos ist. Verdichtet, gekühlt und parfümiert wird das Gas in die Pipelines geschickt. Auf dem langen Weg bis zum Endverbraucher sorgen alle 100 Kilometer Kompressorstationen für die richtige Reisegeschwindigkeit. Für die knapp 3.700 Kilometer lange Strecke von den Förderstätten im Autonomen Kreis der Jamal-Nenzen bis nach Mitteleuropa braucht das Gas sieben bis zwölf Tage.

Gearbeitet wird auf UKPG-2S rund um die Uhr. Von der Chefetage bis zum Facharbeiter arbeiten alle nach der *wachtowy metod*, das heißt im Schichtwechsel: zwölf Stunden am Tag oder zwölf Stunden in der Nacht, ohne Sonn- und Feiertage, einen Monat lang oder neun Stunden pro Tag, sechs Tage am Stück für sechs Wochen. Ganz einfach lässt es sich auch so sagen:

„Wenn wir hier sind, im Schichtdienst, ist immer Montag, jeder Tag Montag. Zu Hause angekommen, ist immer Samstag und Sonntag, so ist die Einteilung!"

Während der Arbeitsperioden wohnen 4.000 Mitarbeiter in der Siedlung Nowosapoljarny, die 2001 ganz in der Nähe der Aufbereitungsanlagen errichtet wurde. Entlang eines großzügigen Boulevards reihen sich dreistöckige Wohngebäude mit rosa-gelb gestrichener Fassade. Gusseiserne Straßenlaternen beleuchten mit fahlem Licht die Straße. Banner und Plakate, nicht mehr im sozialistischen Rot der Sowjetunion, sondern in Gazprom-Blau, aber nicht weniger patriotisch, schmücken die Bauten.

Energie, die Lebensader Russlands!
Hoch leben die Leistungen der Gasarbeiter!
Ruhm der Arbeit!
Sapoljarnoje: 130 Milliarden Kubikmeter Gas im Jahr!

Die Mehrzahl der Arbeiter ist in zwei identischen Wohnkomplexen untergebracht. Beide betritt man über eine großzügige Eingangshalle mit vielen Pflanzen und Aquarien, einem Aufenthaltsbereich mit Sitzgruppe, Flachbildfernseher und zahllosen Geldautomaten. Von hier aus gelangt man in die Kantine, ein Billardzimmer, einen Sportsaal, das Fitnessstudio oder direkt in die Schlaftrakte. Die Ein- und Zweibettzimmer entlang endloser Gänge sind alle gleich eingerichtet: kleine Küche, Duschbad, Bett, Schrank, Fernseher, Bücherbord. Die Ausstattung ist nicht luxuriös, aber man hat auch nicht gespart. Nur wenige Accessoires lassen erkennen, ob hier Frauen oder Männer leben. Aber eigentlich wird hier auch nicht gelebt, sondern ausschließlich geschlafen.

In der Schichtarbeitersiedlung ist alles streng reglementiert. Die Mitarbeiter dürfen die Siedlung nicht verlassen, dürfen keinen Besuch von Freunden oder Verwandten empfangen. Zapfenstreich ist um 22 Uhr, Alkoholkonsum ist auf dem ganzen Gelände strengstens verboten. Zahlreiche Ordnungshüter, meist Frauen, sorgen in den Wohnmodulen dafür, dass diese Regeln eingehalten werden.

Zum Leben erwacht die Siedlung nur morgens und abends beim Schichtwechsel. Hausmeister haben die Treppenstufen zu den Häusern gefegt, der Neuschnee ist beseitigt. Ingenieure und Techniker, Kantinenpersonal und Wachleute eilen zu den blauen Firmenbussen, die sie zu ihrem Arbeitsplatz bringen. Bei Temperaturen um 50 Grad unter Null geht keiner längere Strecken zu Fuß. Bis auf die laufenden Motoren ist es still. Bei diesen Minusgraden tut selbst das Sprechen weh.

Der Winter ist lang, 284 Tage im Jahr. Die Tage im Dezember und Januar sind extrem kurz, der kürzeste Tag dauert gerade mal eine Stunde und ein paar Minuten. Aber der *dlinny rubl*, der „lange Rubel", lockt Tausende junger Frauen und Männer, trotz dieser klimatisch extremen Bedingungen, auf die Gasfelder von Gazprom. Auch den 33-jährigen Ais, Vater von drei Kindern, hat es aus den südlichen Steppen Kalmykiens, nahe des Kaspischen Meeres, an den Polarkreis gezogen. Ais arbeitet als Chauffeur in der Siedlung Nowosapoljarny. Voller Begeisterung spricht er von seiner Arbeit.

„Diese Arbeit schafft hohes Ansehen und der Verdienst ist gut, bemerkenswert gut, den findest du kaum irgendwo. Ich habe Kinder, einen Jungen und zwei Mädchen – ich muss doch in jedem Fall meine Familie ernähren. Und das Sozialpaket ist klasse, kostenlose Reisen ans Schwarze Meer mit Kuraufenthalt, auch für die Kinder, und Prämien!"

Exakte Angaben über die Höhe der Gehälter macht keiner der Gazprom-Mitarbeiter, auch in der Zentrale in Nowy Urengoi gibt es keine Zahlen. Aber alle Befragten bestätigen, dass das Gratifikationspaket, also Gehalt plus Sonderleistungen, erheblich höher ist als der Verdienst im restlichen Russland. Wie alle großen Unternehmen weltweit versucht auch Gazprom, seine Mitarbeiter durch hohe Löhne und Prämien an den Konzern zu binden. Diese Rechnung scheint aufzugehen.

„In der Werbung im Fernsehen hört man oft, dass Gazprom Träume wahr werden lässt. Und das ist wirklich so. Berufliche Fortbildung, ein großzügiges Sozialpaket, Urlaub im Ausland, Gesundheitsvorsorge – das alles bietet Gazprom. Für mich und meine Kollegen ist Gazprom wirklich eine Familie, die uns eint, liebt, sich um uns kümmert in sozialer, finanzieller und kultureller Hinsicht."

Dass der Erdgasriese zum Exportmonopolisten ausgebaut wurde und als politisches Werkzeug dient, spielt für die Gazprom-Familie keine Rolle.

Der 26-jährige Artemi aus Tjumen pendelt schon seit fünf Jahren als Elektroingenieur auf das Erdgasfeld Sapoljarnoje. Das fest geregelte Leben am Polarkreis gefällt dem Vater zweier Kinder. Statt über Kälte und Dunkelheit zu klagen, schätzt er die warme, freundschaftliche Atmosphäre, die ihm Schutz und Sicherheit gibt.

„Noch als Student habe ich verschiedene Praktika gemacht. Ich habe in verschiedenen Betrieben gearbeitet, habe Erfahrungen gesammelt und konnte so gut vergleichen. Mir hat es hier am besten gefallen. Die Tätigkeiten sind interessanter als anderswo – für mich ist es der beste Arbeitsplatz. Wir sind hier zwar am Ende der Welt, doch alles ist vorhanden!"

Für den „Mikrochef", wie sich Artemi nennt, läuft auf den Gasfeldern von Gazprom alles auf Kurs, doch er will noch höher hinaus. Auf die Frage, was er ändern würde, wenn er könnte, antwortet er pragmatisch.

„Gazprom ist ein verhältnismäßig konservatives Unternehmen und revolutionäre Veränderungen sind, so meine ich, nicht angebracht. Es reicht, wenn wir die neuen Standards in der

Gasgewinnung berücksichtigen und zeitgemäße Arbeitsbedingungen erfüllen, wenn wir die neuen Anforderungen der Ökologie und Technik umsetzen. Ich würde hier gern noch lange arbeiten und eine kleine Spur in diesem Riesenunternehmen hinterlassen, hier im Norden. So wie die Männer, die das hier aufgebaut haben. Die waren schon bewundernswert mutig, willensstark und geduldig. Ein klein wenig möchte ich ihnen ähnlich werden. Doch das kostet Kraft!"

Zentraler Treffpunkt der Siedlung ist das Sport- und Kulturzentrum, der gigantische Bau wurde 2011 errichtet. In dem Schwimmbecken von 25 Meter Länge kann man mit Blick in die weiße Polarlandschaft seine Bahnen ziehen, in der Fußball- und Volleyballhalle werden Turniere zwischen den verschiedenen Abteilungen ausgetragen. In der Sauna, beim Tischtennis, Billard oder Darts bietet sich die Gelegenheit zum kameradschaftlichen Beisammensein. Es entsteht der Eindruck, dass es am 66. Breitengrad gelungen ist, Natur und extremes Klima auszutricksen. Aber es ist dann doch beruhigend zu hören, dass hin und wieder auch hier die Planer passen müssen. Die Langlaufloipe – die neuste Attraktion für Wintersportenthusiasten – konnte im vergangenen Jahr erst im April eingeweiht werden, weil bis dahin die Temperaturen nicht über minus 25 Grad gestiegen waren. Und bei dieser Temperatur dürfen nicht einmal die Härtesten in die Loipe, das gefährdet die Gesundheit.

„Natürlich steht bei unserem Sportangebot die Gesundheit unserer Leute an erster Stelle. Das Training soll sie noch fitter machen. Denn die Anpassungen hier sind schwer, zum Beispiel der Wechsel des Biorhythmus, die weiten Entfernungen von zu Hause, die Tag- und Nachtarbeit. Aber Sport hilft dabei, die großen Belastungen besser zu bewältigen, hilft physisch und emotional, die Schicht ohne große Tiefs durchzuhalten."

So erklären es Boris und Kostja, zwei der vielen Trainer und Sporttherapeuten der Siedlung. Wird dennoch ein Mitarbeiter krank, dann kümmert sich ein Heer von Medizinern um den Patienten. Ausgerüstet ist der medizinische Trakt von Nowosapoljarny nicht schlechter als ein normales Kreiskrankenhaus in Westeuropa.

Für alle, die einfach nur einen ruhigen Ort nach Dienstschluss suchen, gibt es den Wintergarten. Er übertrifft alles. Hier wachsen Hunderte weißer und rosafarbener Orchideen, Bougainvilleen und Mandelbäumchen blühen, kleine Zitronen und Mandarinen reifen an zierlichen Bäumen. Die Erde dampft. Und mitten durch diese subtropische Pracht nördlich vom Polarkreis plätschert ein Bächlein. Frösche und Schildkröten tummeln sich im Wasser. Gazproms heile Welt in der Eiswüste.

„Neun Monate im Jahr Winter! Da sehnt sich der Mensch nach Grün, nach dem Sommer. Dann kommst du hierher: ein Garten, Blumen blühen und so ein Duft – das hebt die Stimmung, dir wird leicht ums Herz."

Das bringt nicht nur den Gärtner ins Schwärmen. In dieser grünen Polaridylle ist auch Kristina oft anzutreffen. Außer dem „langen Rubel" hat sie vor allem die Neugierde an den Polarkreis getrieben.

„Ich wollte unbedingt hierher, ich wollte wissen, wie es sich anfühlt, wenn 24 Stunden lang die Sonne scheint, wollte das Polarlicht erleben, wollte Rentiere sehen und die Zelte der Nenzen. Am Anfang war ich so begeistert, ich konnte gar nicht schlafen."

Die 23-Jährige kommt aus Saransk, der Hauptstadt Mordowiens. Kristina gehört zu dem neunköpfigen Team, das mit einem Kulturprogramm Abwechslung in den Alltag am Polarkreis bringt. Es gibt einen Chor, eine Theater- und Tanzgruppe, einen Filmclub. Für

Veranstaltungen steht ein großer Saal mit 230 Sitzplätzen und neuester Beleuchtungs- und Tontechnik zur Verfügung. Kristina entwirft und gestaltet die Kulissen und Kostüme für die Shows. Sie dekoriert die Disco, in der jeden Samstag der Eisbär steppt. Mit dem Geld, das sie hier verdient, finanziert sie ihr Fernstudium zur Kunsterzieherin.

Kristina scheint nicht recht in diese raue Polarlandschaft hineinzupassen. Sie ist ganz schmal, federleicht und trägt auch im Dienst Jeans und Holzfällerhemd. Vor zwei Jahren ist sie nach Nowosapoljarny gekommen, seitdem hat sie viele interessante Menschen kennengelernt. Das strenge Regime nimmt sie leicht.

„Hier gibt es einen ganz geregelten Tagesablauf. Wir dürfen nachts nicht mehr spazieren gehen, nach 22 Uhr nicht mehr das Haus verlassen. Nun, was heißt ‚wir dürfen nicht' – es wird empfohlen, nicht mehr das Haus zu verlassen. Vielleicht ist das bei diesem extremen Klima ja auch richtig, sind Regeln ja auch gut. Aber was soll man machen, wenn die Seele singt!"

Bei Ljoscha lag eine Karriere bei Gazprom auf der Hand. Wie viele seiner Kollegen stammt er aus einer Gasarbeiter-Dynastie. Seine Eltern und seine Schwester haben schon auf dem Feld von Sapoljarnoje gearbeitet. Im Alter von 21 Jahren hat auch Ljoscha seinen Dienst bei Gazprom angetreten, seit sieben Jahren ist er hier nun als Schlosser angestellt. Zuvor hatte er sich bei der Luftwaffe ausprobiert.

„Drei Jahre habe ich gedient. Entscheidend für den Wechsel waren, wie wohl bei den meisten, finanzielle Gründe. Die Bedingungen hier sind gut, die Arbeit ist interessant. Was man verbessern könnte? Der Einfluss der Gewerkschaften könnte größer sein. Und noch mehr Gehalt! Das ist wohl überall die brennendste Frage."

Nach anfänglichen antigewerkschaftlichen Kampagnen wurde vor 15 Jahren die konzerngebundene Gewerkschaft Gazprom Profsojus gegründet. Ljoscha ist Mitglied, wie über 80 Prozent der Mitarbeiter von Gazprom. Für die Gewerkschaft eigentlich eine traumhafte Akzeptanz als Arbeitnehmervertretung. Allerdings ist von der Gazprom-Gewerkschaft nicht bekannt, dass sie sich als moderne, schlagkräftige Organisation etablieren konnte und sich für die Belange der Belegschaft eingesetzt hätte. Wie andere konzerngebundene Gewerkschaften lehnt sie radikale Maßnahmen ab und strebt vielmehr ein freundschaftliches Verhältnis zum Arbeitgeber an, der wiederum die Gewerkschaft moralisch und finanziell unterstützt.

Für die meisten sind nicht die andauernde Kälte und Dunkelheit oder der strikt geregelte Alltag das Härteste am Leben und Arbeiten im Norden, sondern die lange Trennung von der Familie und den Freunden. Auch wenn über Skype, Facebook und Twitter die Liebsten aus der Ferne etwas näher rücken, ist die Sehnsucht unendlich groß.

„Das Schwierigste hier ist, dass die geliebte Frau nicht an deiner Seite ist! Ich habe meine Frau hier kennengelernt, eine Schichtwechsel-Romanze, eine große Liebe."

So wie Ljoscha vermisst auch Artemi seine Familie. Auch er kann das Wiedersehen kaum erwarten. Besonders dieses Ende der Schicht sehnt der frischgebackene Vater brennend herbei. Seinem neugeborenen Sohn konnte er bisher nur durch die Webcam zuwinken. Auf den Arm nehmen wird er seinen Prachtburschen, wie er ihn jetzt schon nennt, erst in ein paar Tagen.

„Kurz vor der Abfahrt nach Hause ist man in einer leichten Euphorie! Es kommt von der Begeisterung, dass du die Schicht überstanden hast, dass du gute Arbeit geleistet hast. Und natürlich vom Wunsch, bald deine Lieben zu sehen. Er wächst ins Unermessliche."

Nach den Wochen intensiver Arbeit geht es für die Gasarbeiter endlich nach Hause, für die meisten *na zemlju*, auf die Große Erde. Vier bis sechs Wochen lang erholen sie sich, in einem milderen Klima, im Kreis der Familie. Dann steht erneut ein Abschied bevor, es geht wieder zur Schicht an den Polarkreis.

Seit vielen Jahren führen auch Eduard Kondratjew und seine Frau Lena eine Beziehung im Monatsrhythmus, seit zwölf Jahren pendelt er aus Nowy Urengoi in die Schichtarbeitersiedlung Nowosapoljarny. So sehr er seine Arbeit in der Schneewüste liebt, die ständig wiederkehrende Trennung von der Familie fällt auch ihm, immer noch, sehr schwer.

„Nun, es ist einfach schwierig, nicht an der Seite deines geliebten Menschen zu sein. Es ist schrecklich, dass du die Entwicklung deines Kindes nicht miterleben, das Kind nicht erziehen kannst, nicht bei den Hausaufgaben hilfst. Das ist bitter und tut wirklich weh."

Während Eduard auf dem Gasfeld arbeitet, lebt Lena zusammen mit der jüngsten Tochter Katja in Nowy Urengoi – eigentlich nicht weit weg vom Arbeitsplatz ihres Mannes und doch unerreichbar fern. Noch nie hat Lena in all den Jahren Eduard an seinem Arbeitsplatz besucht.

Die Familie Kondratjew wohnt in einer Eigentumswohnung in einem Plattenbau, wie die meisten hier, in einer der reichsten Städte Russlands. Bis zum Umbau des Wirtschaftssystems standen die Wohnungen zu moderaten Mietpreisen zur Verfügung, später wurde es möglich, diese als Eigentum zu erwerben – und das zu keinem Schnäppchenpreis: Um die 1.500 Euro kostet ein Quadratmeter Wohnfläche am Polarkreis.

Die Wohngebäude in der Stadt stehen in krassem Gegensatz zur modernen Technologie in der Erdgasförderung. Die Plattenbauten sind mitgenommen, die schneidende Kälte hat deutliche Spuren hinterlassen. Den Wohnhäusern fehlt eine angemessene Wärmedämmung. Die Treppenhäuser sind dunkel, feucht und heruntergekommen, viele Briefkästen im Eingangsbereich sind zerbeult und aufgebrochen, die Wände beschmiert. Ein Niemandsland, für das sich keiner verantwortlich fühlt.

Hinter einer schweren Eisentür dann das gemütliche Paradies der Kondratjews. Die standardisierte Drei-Zimmer-Wohnung haben sie in ein modernes, farbenfrohes Heim verwandelt – bestens ausgestattet mit TV-Flachbildschirm, Stereoanlage, Computer-Ecke, Kochfeld, Geschirrspüler und Whirlpool im Bad. Der Temperaturunterschied zwischen drinnen und draußen beträgt nicht selten unglaubliche 70 Grad. Die zentralgesteuerte Gasheizung hält die Innentemperatur bei wohligen 25 Grad, und das zu einem Fixpreis! Zum Regulieren wird das Fenster geöffnet. Ein sparsamer Umgang mit Rohstoffen und Energie steht in der Erdgashauptstadt nicht an vorderster Stelle.

„Wir haben uns an Nowy Urengoi gewöhnt. Wenn wir in den Urlaub fahren, zieht es uns nach einer Weile wieder hierher zurück. Diese Stadt ist mein Zuhause, obwohl ich nicht hier geboren bin. Mein Vater ist in den Norden gegangen, um zu arbeiten, er hat sich eingerichtet und hat dann seine Familie geholt. Als ich ankam, war ich erstaunt, wie viele junge Leute hier lebten, wie viele Kinder. Alle waren irgendwie besonders, so offen und herzlich."

Sehr genau erinnert sich Lena Kondratjewa daran, wie sie als junges Mädchen zusammen mit ihrer Familie aus Chișinău, im heutigen Moldawien, nach Nowy Urengoi gezogen ist. Über das Besondere an den Menschen hier, über den gutmütigen *sewerny tschelowek*, den „Nordbewohner", hört man am Polarkreis viel.

„Auf der Großen Erde leben die Menschen sicherlich entspannter: Wärme, Wein, Blumen und das Meer. Die Menschen dort sind anders. Unsere Erziehung ist eine eigene, eine des Nordens. Hier sind die Menschen enger zusammengerückt, sie leben freundschaftlicher miteinander."

Der „Nordbewohner" sei offen, sehr hilfsbereit und kameradschaftlich, erklärt Eduard weiter. Über den Grund dieser Besonderheit lässt sich nur mutmaßen. Wahrscheinlich, weil es einfach schwer ist, im hohen Norden allein zu sein.

Wenn Katja trotz bitterer Kälte die Wohnung verlässt, geht sie gerne ins Gudzon. Die Mall, ein zweistöckiger Glaspalast, ist eines von mehreren Einkaufszentren in Nowy Urengoi. Hier reihen sich riesige Elektronik- und Spielwarengeschäfte an die Filialen bekannter Modegeschäfte und Parfümerien, wie es sie auch in vielen europäischen Großstädten gibt. Der Supermarkt ist hervorragend bestückt: von frischer Pasta bis zu Überraschungseiern, von Kefir bis zu französischem Cognac, von Papaya und Kiwis bis hin zu Produkten aus biologischem Anbau. Die Einwohner der Stadt nutzen die zahlreichen Einkaufsmöglichkeiten, doch darüber hinaus ist es ruhig. In den Cafés und Restaurants sind viele Plätze nicht besetzt. Nur wenige, die einen Schaufensterbummel machen. Keine Musikanten und natürlich keine Obdachlosen oder Betrunkenen. Auch Jugendliche, die sich hier einfach die Zeit vertreiben, sind kaum zu sehen. Verwunderlich, da doch die Temperaturen neun lange Monate ein Leben im Freien verbieten, das Spazieren auf den Boulevards, das Liegen im Park oder am Ufer des Flusses unmöglich machen. Auch die Spielplätze sind tief verschneit. Da böte sich doch der Raum unter den Dächern der Einkaufszentren nahezu an, ihn sich anzueignen, ihn zum Treffpunkt zu machen.

Diejenigen, die sich für Singen, Tanzen, Theater oder Sport begeistern, können ihre Freizeit im Sport- und Kulturkomplex „Erdgasarbeiter", geleitet von der Kulturabteilung von Gazprom Dobycha Urengoi, verbringen. Das Angebot ist vielseitig. Der von Gazprom gesponserte Volleyballverein „Fackel" trägt hier seine Heimspiele aus. Zu großen Festen, Konzerten oder Aufführungen sind die Ränge des Veranstaltungssaals gefüllt. Wer in der Erdgashauptstadt auftritt und die Einwohner unterhält, das bestimmt allerdings Gazprom. Dem Unterhaltungsprogramm seien strikte Grenzen gesetzt, bedauert eine Mitarbeiterin der Theatergruppe. Jedes Vorhaben, jeder Gastauftritt müsse von der Kulturabteilung abgesegnet werden.

In der Mall, im großen Sport- und Kulturzentrum und in den anderen Freizeiteinrichtungen scheint alles organisiert und gesteuert. Vielleicht sind die eigenen vier Wände der einzige Ort, an dem sich die Menschen ihr Leben selbst einrichten können – wo die Regeln des Erdgaskonzerns draußen bleiben müssen? Jedenfalls nennen sehr viele Bewohner von Nowy Urengoi als Lieblingsort in der Stadt ihr eigenes Heim.

„Mein Lieblingsplatz in der Stadt? Natürlich mein Haus! Als Kind war die Wohnung meiner Eltern der schönste Ort auf der Welt, heute habe ich mein eigenes, gemütliches Nest!"

Doch egal, ob die Freizeit mit Familie und Freunden in der Stadt oder auch einfach nur zu Hause genossen wird, der Alltag in Nowy Urengoi steht unter dem Stern der Arbeit und der Raum für Muße ist begrenzt. Das trifft nicht weniger auf die jungen Einwohner zu, denn schon die Jugendlichen sind dazu aufgefordert, sich in Strebsamkeit und Fleiß zu üben.

Wie auf viele Lebensbereiche nimmt die Erdgasbranche auch Einfluss auf die Ausbildung, besonders Gazprom investiert viel in den Nachschub an jungen Spezialisten. Im nördlichen Teil der Stadt befindet sich die Fachhochschule der Erdgasindustrie, errichtet und finanziert von Gazprom. Hier werden ungefähr 1.000 Schüler vier Jahre lang in der Technik der Erdgasförderung, aber auch in Betriebswirtschaft und Buchhaltung ausgebildet. Ein fester Bestandteil des Lehrplans sind Praktika in dem großen Konzern. Neben besten Fachkenntnissen seien Teamgeist, Anpassungsfähigkeit, Stressresistenz, Verantwortungsbewusstsein und Ehrlichkeit gefragt, erklärt der Pressesprecher Sergei Tschernezki.

„Wir sind kein Wohltätigkeitsverein, wir nehmen nur die Besten. Aber es ist nicht so, dass wir einfach nur Goldfischchen aus dem Teich fangen können. Wir investieren einiges, um Mitarbeiter zu werben und zu behalten. In letzter Zeit sind viele, nein, nicht viele, sondern einige Mitarbeiter in unabhängige Unternehmen gewechselt, weil sie dort wohl mehr verdienen."

An den größten technischen Universitäten des Landes, in Ufa, Kasan, Krasnodar, Tjumen oder Moskau und St. Petersburg organisiert Gazprom regelmäßig Informationsveranstaltungen und lädt die Interessenten zu einem Gespräch in die Erdgashauptstadt ein, um ihnen die Aussicht auf einen gesicherten und gut bezahlten Arbeitsplatz schmackhaft zu machen. Aber die Bemühungen um die Personalbeschaffung setzen schon früher an, sie beginnen bereits in der Schule. Der Konzern Gazprom versucht besonders begabte Schülerinnen und Schüler zu fördern und sie schon in jungen Jahren als potentielle Mitarbeiter für sich zu gewinnen.

Der 16-jährige Dima ist Fan deutscher Rockmusik und Schüler der Gazprom-Klasse des städtischen Gymnasiums in Nowy Urengoi. Sie ist erst im letzten Jahr eingerichtet worden. Der Klassenraum ist in den Konzernfarben gestrichen und mit modernster Technik ausgestattet, über der interaktiven Tafel prangt das Fackel-Logo. Hier werden die Besten der Besten auf eine mögliche Arbeit im Betrieb vorbereitet.

Wenn es ab minus 40 Grad mal wieder Kältefrei gibt, können die Schüler die Aufgaben zu Hause über das Internet abfragen und per Mausklick die Lösungen an die Schule schicken. Wie alle Schüler freuen sich Dima und seine Klassenkameraden, wenn der Unterricht ausfällt. An solchen Tagen, und die gibt es hier am Polarkreis gar nicht selten, können sie ausschlafen. Ganz normale Schüler also, nur wissen sie im Alter von 16 Jahren schon ziemlich genau, was sie einmal werden wollen und warum.

„Wer in der Gazprom-Klasse ist, kann mehr lernen, einfach deshalb, weil Fachleute besondere Vorlesungen halten, die andere Schüler nicht hören. Außerdem ist es eine große Chance, in der Zukunft für Gazprom zu arbeiten. Das ist eine großartige Perspektive! Das Gehalt ist sicher und hoch. Das ist der Weg in eine große Zukunft."

Mehr als 50.000 Euro kostet eine Gazprom-Klasse im Jahr, und es soll solche Klassen in naher Zukunft in ganz Russland geben, um für den dringend benötigten Nachwuchs zu sorgen. Doch Gazprom ist nicht nur für Spezialisten in der Erdgasindustrie ein hoch geschätzter Arbeitgeber. Nahezu jeder Bewohner von Nowy Urengoi äußert sich positiv über eine Anstellung bei Gazprom.

„Du bist stolz, sagen zu können, dass du bei Gazprom arbeitest."

Tatjana Borisowna spricht im Namen ihres Kindergartenteams. Von den zahlreichen Kindergärten in der Stadt unterhält der Erdgaskonzern acht eigene, zwei mit dem besonderen Profil: „Prophylaxe". Das sind Belosneschka, „Schneewittchen", im Süden und Morosko, „Väterchen Frost", im Norden der Stadt. Kein Kind muss länger als ein paar Minuten zu seinem Kindergarten gehen. Die Stadt tut viel, um in dem menschenfeindlichen Klima ihre Kinder zu schützen und den Mangel an Bewegungsmöglichkeiten im Freien auszugleichen: Sporthallen und Schwimmbassins wurden in die Kindergärten integriert und Wald und Feld im Miniformat als Wintergärten angelegt, und zwar in jedem Kindergarten der Stadt. Doch Gazprom tut noch mehr.

In Morosko, er wurde als bester Kindergarten Russlands ausgezeichnet, kümmern sich insgesamt 72 Erzieherinnen, Köchinnen und Küchenhilfen, HNO- und Kinderärzte, Sprach- und Physiotherapeutinnen um das Wohlergehen von 220 Kindern.

„Die medizinische Vorsorge unserer Kinder ist sehr wichtig. Das Klima im Norden greift die Gesundheit von Kindern und Erwachsenen an. Die Bedingungen sind hier ja extrem."

Eine Augenärztin überprüft die Sehschärfe und verordnet die richtige Brille. Logopäden korrigieren die Aussprache. Masseurinnen kümmern sich um die verhärteten Muskeln der Anderthalbjährigen. Nach dem Saunagang wird den Kleinen an gedeckten Tischchen ein Tee serviert, danach geht es in die Gruppenräume, die bis an die Decke mit Spielzeug gefüllt sind. Und das I-Tüpfelchen, das diesen Kindergarten zum allerbesten macht, ist die Salzkammer: In einem abgedunkelten Raum, dessen Wände und Decke einer Felsgrotte gleichen, liegen die Kinder mit Mütze und Handschuhen in Bettchen, schauen Trickfilme und atmen dabei Luft, die mit Salz und anderen Zusatzstoffen angereichert ist, um einer Lungenentzündung vorzubeugen. Nach der Behandlung gibt es noch einen schaumigen Drink.

„Wir hier im Norden kämpfen mit Sauerstoffmangel. Und deshalb bekommen unsere Kinder einen Sauerstoffcocktail, um das, was fehlt, zu ergänzen."

Willkommen im „Raumschiff Morosko"! Über die Notwendigkeit des Getränks lässt sich freilich streiten – oder auch einfach die Wissenschaft befragen. Russische wie deutsche Experten bestätigen, dass der Sauerstoffgehalt am Polarkreis nicht niedriger ist als sonst wo auf der Welt. Doch die Mär vom Sauerstoffmangel gehört zum Leben im hohen Norden dazu.

„Unsere Armee ist stark, so stark, unsere Armee ist kühn, so kühn, unsere Armee ist tapfer, so tapfer!" – trällert eine helle Kinderstimme aus den Lautsprechern über die Flure von Morosko zu Ehren des bevorstehenden Feiertags, des Tages der Verteidiger des Vaterlandes. Spätestens die Hymne aus dem Kindermund holt den Besucher aus der vermeintlich sauerstoffarmen Umlaufbahn zurück in die Atmosphäre eines dann doch ganz normalen russischen Kindergartens, in dem schon die Kleinsten lernen sollen, die Armee zu achten und das Heimatland zu lieben.

In das Bestehen von Nowy Urengoi und die Zukunft der Bewohner wird viel investiert. So umfangreich die Vorhaben und groß die Bemühungen aber auch sind, die Vitalität der Stadt ist alternativlos an das Geschäft mit dem Rohstoff geknüpft. Sorgen macht man sich in der Erdgashauptstadt aber nicht. Ausgeschöpfte Lagerstätten und versiegende Quellen sind kein Thema, Nowy Urengoi wird Gazproms wichtiger Außenposten bleiben.

„Klar wird das Gas Jahr für Jahr weniger. In manchen Förderstätten befinden wir uns nun auf dem Höhepunkt, das hält vielleicht noch fünf bis sechs Jahre an. Dann geht dort die Gasförderung zurück, dann werden weiter im Norden neue Gasfelder erschlossen, aber keine neuen Städte gebaut, sondern nur kleine Siedlungen für den Schichtbetrieb. Nowy Urengoi wird der Brückenkopf bleiben."

Von der Erschließung neuer Erdgasfelder sind auch die Nenzen betroffen, nomadische Rentierhirten, Jäger und Fischer, die im Autonomen Kreis der Jamal-Nenzen leben und ihm den Namen gaben. Jede Produktionsstätte ist ein Eingriff in die Natur, der Abbau von Bodenschätzen hat Umweltschäden zur Folge, die auch die indigene Bevölkerung gefährden. Das ist dem Pressesprecher Sergei Tschernezki sehr wohl bewusst, wortreich betont er das gute Verhältnis zwischen den Nenzen und dem Gasgiganten und verweist auf die Maßnahmen, mit denen Gazprom die verbauten Weidegründe der Ureinwohner zu ersetzen versucht. Dazu zählt er die Siedlungen für die Nomaden im Norden der Region, ein vom Konzern gesponsertes Internat und kostenfreie Ausbildungsplätze für Jugendliche. Gern feiere man auch gemeinsam die traditionellen Feste der Nomaden, das Fest des Rentierzüchters oder das des Fischers. Das klingt beinahe wie eine Idylle, ist es aber nicht. Hinter dem vorgeblichen Wohlwollen stehen wirtschaftliche Interessen. Um das lukrative Erdgasgeschäft aufrechtzuerhalten, wird die Industrie dem Rohstoff in immer entlegenere Gebiete folgen – nicht zuletzt bis auf den Grund des Arktischen Ozeans, wo man große Erdgasvorkommen vermutet.

Immer mehr Menschen werden Monat für Monat in den Norden pendeln, um die anhaltende Nachfrage nach dem Rohstoff zu bedienen. Doch nicht nur neue Förderstätten bieten Arbeitsplätze, auch Nowy Urengoi selbst lockt mit gutbezahlten Jobs – ob Ärztin oder Lehrer, Bauarbeiter oder Kellnerin, in der Erdgashauptstadt wird jeder gebraucht. Und die Stadtbaudirektion soll den Lebensstandard aller Bewohner nicht nur sichern, sondern stetig verbessern. Es wird modernisiert und ausgebaut, Schritt für Schritt wird subarktische Landschaft in Stadtgebiet verwandelt.

„Wir haben die schwierige Aufgabe, für Leute, die in sehr alten, beschädigten Häusern leben, neuen Wohnraum zu schaffen. Diese Aufgabe ist wichtig und muss schnell erledigt werden. Die alten Gebäude wurden rasch gebaut, aber für die Schönheit fehlte die Kraft. Heute versuchen wir, den neuen Stadtteilen eine besondere Handschrift zu geben, so dass sie nicht so eintönig sind. Wir beschäftigen uns auch mit der Begrünung, bauen Boulevards und Parkanlagen. Und das alles für eine hohe Lebensqualität in der Stadt."

Im Süden, wo vor kurzem noch einstöckige Holzhäuser und Schuppen aus den Anfangsjahren standen, entsteht das neue Wohnviertel „Tundra". Es unterscheidet sich nicht wesentlich von jenen aus sozialistischer Zeit. Fünf- und neunstöckige Wohnblocks werden, gedreht und gespiegelt, rund um einen großzügigen Innenhof angeordnet. Im Hof ein Kindergarten und eine Schule – bequem zu Fuß erreichbar. Demnächst können 1.400 Familien die neuen Wohnungen beziehen. Der Projektentwickler wirbt mit der fortschrittlichen Bauweise, dem Einsatz einer effizienten Wärmedämmung und mit einer Vielzahl von Parkplätzen. Die sonst übliche Fassade aus vorfabrizierten Betonelementen wird durch eine Verkleidung aus beigen und braunen Platten ersetzt und mit roten Vordächern, Türmchen und Ziergiebeln geschmückt.

Etwas ganz Neues ist die Planung von Einfamilienhaus-Vierteln. Der Trend zum eigenen Haus mit Garten – auch wenn dieser nur wenige Tage im Jahr genutzt werden kann – hat den Polarkreis erreicht.

„In den letzten Jahren hat sich die Situation etwas geändert. Es gibt den Wunsch nach individuellen Wohnhäusern. Das liegt daran, dass die Leute länger in der Stadt bleiben, als man ursprünglich gedacht hat."

Der verantwortliche Stadtplaner ist mit einer neuen Aufgabe betraut: Sowohl im südlichen, als auch im nördlichen Teil der Stadt sieht der Entwicklungsplan Viertel mit Einfamilienhäusern vor. Kaum vorstellbar, dass in Zukunft am Polarkreis Bungalows und Villen stehen, jedes Haus eine Trutzburg in der Schneewüste, versorgt mit Wärme, Wasser und Elektrizität. Doch ohne Zweifel ist auch das in der Gazprom City möglich.

Auch wenn die Bewohner heute nicht nur für ein paar Jahre, sondern für ganze Jahrzehnte in Nowy Urengoi leben, für ewig wollen die Menschen dann doch nicht im hohen Norden bleiben. Spätestens nach ihrer Pensionierung zieht es sie zurück *na zemlju*, auf die Große Erde. Für ein Leben im Alter ist diese Stadt am Polarkreis ohnehin nicht gemacht.

Nach 20 langen Dienstjahren im hohen Norden können Frauen mit 50 in den wohlverdienten Ruhestand gehen, Männer stehen fünf Jahre länger in der Pflicht. Besonders schwere Arbeitsbedingungen verkürzen die Mindestarbeitszeit eventuell um einige Jahre.

„Du arbeitest gewissenhaft und auf hohem Niveau. Und so gehst du erhobenen Hauptes von hier weg. Du verdienst hier unbestritten all das, was du jemals haben wolltest. Du bekommst alles. Du wirst mit Anerkennung, Urkunden, Medaillen ausgezeichnet. Kurzum: Wenn du tüchtig arbeitest, kannst du dich als Rentner auch richtig ausruhen."

So träumen die meisten davon, im Alter aus dieser Stadt wegzuziehen, von einem Leben danach. Und Gazprom hat diesen Traum in seinem Lebensentwurf für die Mitarbeiter eingeplant. Der Konzern bietet ein betriebliches Sparmodell an, mit dem langjährig Wohnraum „in Russland" finanziert wird. Die Mitarbeiter zahlen nur einen kleinen Teil selbst. Sie können sich ganz der Vorstellung widmen, wie das Wunschhaus auszusehen hat. So wird in den langen Wintermonaten an vielen Küchentischen in Nowy Urengoi hin und her überlegt, hier werden schon konkrete Pläne entworfen. Die Mitarbeiter des weltweit größten Erdgasförderunternehmens heben in ihren Träumen nicht ab, stehen vielmehr fest mit beiden Beinen auf heimatlichem Boden.

„Ob ich schon Pläne für die Pension habe? Das Wichtigste ist, ein Haus zu bauen, eine Villa, sie soll auf jeden Fall zwei Etagen haben, so dass mich die Kinder und meine Enkel jederzeit besuchen kommen können und jeder seine kleine Ecke hat. Ich werde einen großen Hund im Haus haben und draußen einen Wachhund. Ja, zwei Hunde werden wir haben und eine Katze und ein riesiges Aquarium. Ich will einen Garten anlegen mit Blumen, Büschen, Beeren, keinen Kartoffelacker! Wo man einen Tisch und Stühle hinstellen kann, einen Samowar, und abends trinkt man Tee, die Kinder rennen umher und wenn es warm ist, kann man im Pool schwimmen. Und irgendwo steht da ein Grill und die ganze Familie kommt zusammen. Es muss so gemütlich sein, dass alle immer wieder gern nach Hause kommen wollen."

В начале февраля мы летим самолетом российской авиакомпании S7 Airlines из Москвы в Новый Уренгой — российскую газовую столицу в западной Сибири. Все места на рейс распроданы. На борту почти нет пожилых пассажиров, а молодые явно не экипированы для полярной экспедиции. Только мы потеем в пуховиках и меховых сапогах. Почти три с половиной часа длится полёт, и на протяжении почти всего времени тянется снежная пустыня, которая кажется бесконечной. Иногда в рассветном воздухе появляются очертания маленького посёлка или пламя газового факела.

Без дружеского участия сотрудницы Газпрома Гульназ Колоколовой и без пропуска, позволяющего преодолевать все барьеры и удостоверяющего, что мы являемся гостями Газпрома, наше путешествие закончилось бы еще на паспортном контроле. Город закрыт для иностранцев и для его посещения требуется особое разрешение, выданное газовым концерном. Мы посылали бесчисленные запросы и неутомимо спрашивали и переспрашивали, пока наконец в московском главном офисе нам не дали зелёный свет.

Что же заставило нас пуститься в путешествие к этому городу, лежащему недалеко от Полярного Круга, в котором больше крупных индустриальных объектов, чем достопримечательностей, а климат никак не назовешь приветливым?

Взаимная зависимость Европы и России от импорта и экспорта газа и весомая позиция Газпрома — частая тема в политике и средствах массовой информации. Последствия этой зависимости для потребителей в Европе, на другом конце газопровода, выносятся на первый план. Производство работ и связанные с этим условия жизни людей, работающих у месторождений в западной Сибири, обсуждаются, напротив, гораздо реже.

Как живут люди в Новом Уренгое — в городе, который абсолютно зависим от газовых ресурсов и где ритм жизни целиком и полностью подчинён нуждам газового концерна?

На стоянке перед аэропортом цифровое табло показывает минус 45 градусов по Цельсию. В считанные секунды индевеют очки, больно дышать. Водитель, предоставленный Газпромом, уже ожидает нас и везёт в гостиницу «Полярная Звезда». В предстоящие десять дней мы хотим познакомиться с газовой столицей и насколько это возможно погрузиться в будни города.

Вдали от Большой земли
ГОЛОСА ИЗ ГОРОДА В ПРИПОЛЯРЬЕ

«Город Новый Уренгой существует только потому, что здесь расположено Уренгойское газовое месторождение. Если бы тут не обнаружили залежи газа, города бы не было. Наш город называют еще „газовой столицей“ или просто — Газпром Сити».

Почти 50 лет назад в Западной Сибири было открыто множество связанных между собой малых месторождений, которые образуют одно из самых больших газовых месторождений на земле — Уренгойское. Вдалеке от человеческого жилья, среди болотистых озёр субарктической тундры, началось плановое развитие газовой промышленности. Чтобы принять участие в великой стройке, большое число добровольцев приехало в этот суровый край, где с сентября по май температура воздуха опускается ниже нуля, при этом морозы достигают нередко минус 50 градусов. Началось строительство транспортных путей, были проложены сотни километров трубопроводов, налажены буровые установки и, шаг за шагом, маленький посёлок для рабочих превратился в северную метрополию Новый Уренгой.

Эдуарду Кондратьеву было 8 лет, когда его родители с тремя детьми переехали в середине 70-х с Юга России в Приполярье, чтобы вместе с тысячами других рабочих включиться в газовую разработку и заработать денег.

«Я еще очень хорошо помню все, что тогда было. У меня остались неизгладимые впечатления, которые сопровождают меня на протяжении всей моей жизни. Они так сильны, что из-за них я, возможно, никогда не уеду отсюда. Знаете, у Севера есть особый дух! В первые годы мы жили в „бочках“, что-то типа вагончиков на козлах. Часто 2–3 семьи ютились на площади примерно в 15 квадратных метров. Родители утром уезжали на работу, а дети оставались дома с самодельными игрушками из консервных банок. Такие воспоминания, пожалуй, не забываются никогда».

Для строительства города решили выбрать узкую, одиннадцатикилометровую полоску на южной оконечности Уренгойского месторождения, ограниченную двумя притоками реки Пур и окружённую тысячами озёр и болотец, которые зимой исчезают под толстым слоем снега. Рядом с временным жилищем рабочих был вбит столб с символической доской с именем города. На памяти Эдуарда скудные деревянные хибары уступили место высотным панельным домам, строились городские дороги и жилые кварталы, в мёрзлой земле прокладывались коммуникации, чтобы обеспечить жителей светом и теплом.

По правилам советского градостроительства, план города был быстро набросан на кульмане. Вдоль магистрали были возведены стандартные жилые блоки, с внутренними дворами и расположенными в них городскими учреждениями типа школы или детского сада. Ленинградский строительный комбинат № 3 поставлял готовые бетонные блоки для жилых домов, на Север шли панели типа 1-ЛГ-600. Дома 600-ой серии назывались «кораблями», потому что длинные, горизонтальные оконные рамы напоминали океанский лайнер.

Все дома похожи друг на друга, их можно отличить только по цвету фасадов. Несколько строений образуют жилые кварталы, так называемые микрорайоны. Им присваиваются звучные имена: микрорайон «Оптимистов», «Энтузиастов», «Дорожников» или просто «Полярный» и «Солнечный». Между кварталами находятся больница, административные здания и места для культурного отдыха. Городского центра, как такового, нет. Когда жилья стало не хватать, город начал разрастаться на другой стороне реки. Там была построен район под названием Северка с микрорайонами «Дружба», «Мирный», «Советский» и «Юбилейный».

Сегодня Новый Уренгой является благоустроенным мегаполисом с населением более 110 тыс. человек, причём добрые три четверти российского газа добываются здесь, в сложной системе бурового оборудования, которое поставляет и контролирует концерн Газпром. Большинство жителей работают на газодобыче в Газпроме или в одном из его бесчисленных дочерних предприятий и фирмах-партнёрах.

Эдуард, которому сейчас 44 года, вспоминает начало своей карьеры в Газпроме. В течение многих лет он выполнял различные работы. В данный момент он занимает должность ведущего инженера в компании Газпром Добыча Ямбург. Эдуарду поступали заманчивые предложения из центрального управления Газпрома в Москве, ему предлагали поработать в столице, однако он решил остаться в Новом Уренгое. По его словам — из любви к Северу. Здесь он познакомился со своей женой Леной, здесь выросли его дети Юрий, Александра и Екатерина. В свободное время он наслаждается тем, что предлагает природа: наблюдением за северными оленями, полярными куропатками и песцами, на которых он не охотится, а фотографирует, а также рыбалкой в кристально-прозрачных реках западно-сибирской тундры.

«Стоит только выглянуть в окно, и ты увидишь, сколько тут прекрасного! Здесь всё огромно — природа, просторы и дали, всё невероятно величественно. Могучая промышленность и высокие технологии. Недра земли полны сокровищами и работе не видно ни конца, ни края».

Многих, в основном молодых людей, Север и сегодня всё ещё притягивает возможностью заработать хорошие деньги в Газпром Сити. Работа на газодобыче обеспечивает надёжный и высокий, по российским меркам, доход. Они согласны жить в самых труднодоступных уголках Земли, полностью посвящая свою жизнь газовой отрасли.

«Когда был основан Новый Уренгой, здесь было одно так называемое градообразующее предприятие — сегодняшний концерн Газпром, который выстроил инфраструктуру города: дороги, детские сады, школы и жилые дома. Сегодня эта ответственность лежит на нас».

А конкретнее, на архитекторе Евгении Ворошилове, главном ответственном градостроителе Нового Уренгоя. Молодой крымчанин три года назад переехал с женой и двумя детьми в Приполярье, чтобы занять пост начальника управления градостроительства и архитектуры. С 2006 года за развитие и контроль всех строительных проектов города отвечает городское управление градостроительства и архитектуры, раньше этим занимался Газпром.

В целом, по словам архитектора, Новый Уренгой функционирует как любой другой город, разве что он расположен в Приполярье. Здесь есть электростанция, завод по сжиганию мусора и водоочистные сооружения. Продукты питания по большей части привозные, а некоторые производятся на месте. Есть хлебозавод, мясокомбинат и большой парник. Город больше не производит свежего молока — это оказалось слишком дорого, коров пришлось переместить в южные регионы. В свободное время можно сходить в кино, в музей истории газовой промышленности или в боулинг «Полярную сову», во Дворец Культуры или в один из нескольких огромных спортивных залов. Здесь есть православная церковь и мечеть. В советские времена сюда приезжали люди самых различных национальностей: русские, белорусы, украинцы, татары, кумыки, азербайджанцы, башкиры, чеченцы.

«Новый Уренгой — город газовиков. Он строился добровольцами с огромным энтузиазмом. Многие внесли свой вклад, добавили что-то новое, подружились. Здесь царит особый дух, который помогает преодолевать суровые условия. Это функциональный город, его архитектура подчинена потребностям. Наш город — памятник труду и тем, кто его основал и открыл газовые месторождения».

С начала разработки Уренгойского месторождения было добыто 6,5 триллионов кубометров газа. Это высочайшее достижение было занесено в книгу рекордов Гиннесса! Никогда ещё такое гигантское количество газа не было выкачано из одного единственного месторождения, и Уренгойское не должно было оставаться единственным в этом газовом Эльдорадо: месторождение Ямбург было разработано в 1986 году, Заполярное — в 2001; Южно-Русское и Береговое соединились в сеть в 2007 году, в 2012 началась разработка Самбургского месторождения. Вести о столь выдающемся успехе выходят далеко за рамки сухой статистики и заголовков газет.

Газпром, русский богатырь!
Планета Газпром
Вперёд, Газпром! Вперёд, Газпром!

Под этими заголовками поются гимны и восхваляются успехи самого большого в мире энергетического концерна. Слова и общий тон напоминают советские патриотические песни рабочих.

С 1992 года Газпром преобразовался в акционерное общество, до этого он подчинялся Министерству нефтяной и газовой промышленности. Государство владеет контрольным пакетом из 50 процентов и одной акции и представляет большинство в совете директоров. Газпром — один из крупнейших работодателей страны и насчитывает около 459 000 сотрудников. Концерн поддерживает российский госбюджет миллиардными вливаниями, является крупнейшим поставщиком валюты в стране и наиважнейшим поставщиком энергоносителей во многие страны Центральной Европы, которые зависят от западносибирского газа. Благодаря открытию новых месторождений в более удалённых районах, Новый Уренгой выполняет теперь функцию плацдарма: город обеспечивает посадку газовикам, отсюда они едут дальше, к своим рабочим местам. 20 000 рабочих посменно трудятся на местах добычи газа вокруг Нового Уренгоя.

Многие курсируют из удалённых регионов России, другие прямиком из газовой столицы. В городе находятся штаб-квартиры компаний Газпром Добыча Ямбург и Газпром Добыча Уренгой. Отсюда осуществляется управление производством и транспортировкой сырья по России и далее заграницу и координируется работа тысяч сотрудников, так необходимых на производстве.

Автобусы с рабочими покидают городской аэропорт и направляются в сторону Заполярного. Место разработки расположено в 220 километрах к северо-востоку от Нового Уренгоя. Вдоль городской границы стоят пропускные пункты: в этом стратегически важном районе проверяют не только иностранцев, но и любого, кто едет из пункта А в пункт В. Если температура опускается ниже минус 45 градусов, автобусы, в целях безопасности, должны следовать колонной. Трасса хорошая, по обе стороны от нее — заснеженный ландшафт. Где-то здесь угадывается извивающаяся в низине река Пур. По берегам стоят берёзы, лиственницы, сибирские кедры и ели. Через некоторое время картина резко меняется: перед нами расстилается безбрежная, белая, снежная пустыня. Взгляду не на чем остановиться: ни возвышенности, ни леса, ни населенного пункта — только горизонт. Оживляют монотонный пейзаж лишь стальные обледенелые столбы и редкие газовые факелы — знак Газпрома.

При экстремально низких температурах и при определённом преломлении солнечных лучей, красочные световые отражения окончательно преобразуют снежную пустыню в сюрреалистическую декорацию. Напротив, очень реалистично на этом фоне выглядят грузовики, внедорожники и автобусы, которые в большом количестве движутся по обледенелой трассе. Невозможно себе представить, но это так: в бесснежные месяцы лета здесь зеленеют растения, расцветает вся тундра, появляются грибы, цветут всевозможные ягодные кустарники и немного позже приносят плоды. Лето длится здесь лишь 35 дней.

В центре безграничного снежного поля, в 60 километрах к северу от полярного круга, расположен УКПГ-2С — один из пяти газоперерабатывающих заводов Заполярного. Только после ещё одного паспортного контроля разрешается пройти на обнесённую ограждением территорию предприятия. Промышленный комплекс состоит из нескольких цехов и километровой трубопроводной системы. Повсюду вокруг газоперерабатывающей фабрики, на глубине до 3 000 метров, залегает газ, который выходит на поверхность через большую, извилистую трубу, приподнятую на козлах в почти безлюдном заводском помещении. Голоса не слышны, раздается лишь монотонный гул и свист машин. Переплетение тонких и толстых цветных труб, турбины, цистерны и аппаратура для измерения количества, плотности, давления и температуры. Ни пота, ни грязи — только хайтек на самом высоком уровне!

«Здесь мы добываем 130 миллиардов кубометров газа в год. Это больше, чем годовой расход газа Германии. Качество этого газа очень высокое, он состоит на 99,8 процента из метана. Примеси пропана, бутана и азота минимальны. Воды в газе тоже не много — всего 200 граммов на тысячу кубометров».

Азат Гумеров, заместитель начальника промысла, работает уже несколько лет на западно-сибирских газовых разработках. Он не без гордости сообщает о высоких достижениях на предприятии, факты и цифры у него наготове.

На территории редко встретишь техника в белой каске и голубой куртке с логотипом Газпрома. Прошли времена, когда в конце прошлого столетия болотистая земля тундры была засыпана метровым слоем песка, прошли времена, когда огромная бурильная головка внедрялась в газовый пласт, выбрасывая на поверхность камни и грязь. Сегодня на предприятии УКПГ-2С царит стерильная чистота. Все операции управляются компьютером. День и ночь два диспетчера отслеживают на больших экранах каждый шаг по переработке газа. Все данные передаются в «сердце», как тут называют Центр контроля. Здесь сотрудники не носят газпромовской униформы, а ходят в тёмных костюмах. Если в этой весьма сложной системе происходят неполадки, загорается предупреждающая красная лампочка. На экране высвечивается, сколько газа было добыто в последние два часа, это количество сравнивается с дневной нормой добычи. Царит непринуждённая атмосфера, молодые мужчины одним глазом посматривают хоккей по телевизору.

Прежде чем газ покинет завод, в него, в целях технической безопасности, вводят ароматизаторы — так называемые одоранты, потому что природный газ не имеет ни цвета, ни запаха. Сжатый, охлаждённый и одорированный газ направляется в трубопроводы. Каждые 100 км, на протяжении долгого пути к потребителю, компрессорные станции регулируют необходимую скорость газового потока. Для преодоления расстояния от места добычи в автономном Ямало-Ненецком округе до Центральной Европы — пути длиной 3 700 километров — требуется от семи до двенадцати дней.

На УКПГ-2С работа ведётся круглосуточно. Все служащие, начиная от руководителей и специалистов и заканчивая квалифицированными рабочими, работают вахтовым методом, то есть посменно: один месяц двенадцать часов днём или в ночь без выходных и праздников, или девять часов в день шесть дней в неделю, на протяжении шести недель. Можно сказать очень просто:

«Когда мы работаем здесь посменно, для нас всегда понедельник, каждый день понедельник. Дома всегда суббота и воскресение, вот такое деление».

Во время рабочей вахты 4 000 работников живут в посёлке Новозаполярный, который был построен совсем рядом с газоперерабатывающим заводом в 2001 году. Вдоль широкого бульвара выстроились трёхэтажные жилые дома с жёлто-розовыми фасадами. Чугунные уличные фонари тускло освещают дорогу. Здания украшают выдержанные в голубых тонах Газпрома баннеры и плакаты, они больше не пестрят красным, как во времена СССР, но выглядят не менее патриотично.

Энергия недр России!
Да здравствуют трудовые достижения газовиков!
Слава труду!
Заполярное: 130 миллиардов кубометров газа в год!

Большинство рабочих расселены в двух одинаковых жилых комплексах. При входе в комплекс вы попадаете в огромный холл, со множеством растений и аквариумов, гостиной с диванами и телевизором с плоским экраном, а также с многочисленными банкоматами. Отсюда можно попасть в столовую, биллиардную, фитнес-студию, спортзал или прямиком в спальное крыло здания. Вдоль бесконечного коридора расположены одно- и двухместные комнаты с одинаковой планировкой: маленькая кухня, душевая кабина, кровать, шкаф, телевизор, книжная полка. Обстановка не шикарная, но и не скудная. Только по некоторым предметам можно догадаться кто тут живёт — женщины или мужчины. Но, собственно говоря, здесь не живут, а практически только спят.

В вахтовом городке жизнь строго регламентирована. Работникам не разрешается покидать посёлок и принимать гостей — будь то друзья или родственники. Отбой в

22:00 часа, употребление алкоголя на всей территории строго запрещено. Многочисленные вахтерши наблюдают за выполнением этих правил в жилых комплексах.

Посёлок оживляется лишь утром и вечером при пересменке. Дворники очищают ведущие к домам ступеньки от выпавшего за ночь снега. Инженеры и техники, работники столовой и охранники спешат к голубым газпромовским автобусам, которые отвозят их к рабочим местам. При температуре около 50 градусов ниже нуля никто не ходит на большие расстояния пешком. Не слышно никаких звуков, кроме гула работающих моторов. При таких низких температурах даже разговаривать больно.

Зима здесь долгая — 284 дня в году. В декабре и январе дни очень коротки, самый короткий день длится один час и пару минут. Но «длинный рубль» манит тысячи молодых женщин и мужчин в эти экстремальные климатические условия, на газовые разработки Газпрома. Айс, 33-летний отец троих детей, также приехал в Заполярье из южных калмыцких степей, что рядом с Каспийским морем. Айс работает водителем в посёлке Новозаполярный и рассказывает о своей работе с восторгом.

«Это престижная работа, она оплачивается очень и очень хорошо, такой заработок вряд ли можно найти где-нибудь ещё. У меня дети, мальчик и две девочки — я же должен кормить свою семью. И соцпакет классный! Бесплатные путевки на Чёрное море для нас и детей, да ещё и премии!»

Точных сведений о зарплатах вам не выдаст ни один сотрудник Газпрома, в штаб-квартире компании в Новом Уренгое вам тоже не дадут таких цифр. Однако все опрошенные подтверждают: полный пакет — оклад плюс льготы — значительно выше, чем заработки на остальной территории России. Газпром, как и все крупные предприятия в мире, старается привязать своих сотрудников к концерну высокими зарплатами и премиями. Похоже, эта тактика работает.

«Часто в телевизионной рекламе можно услышать, что Газпром превращает мечты в реальность. И это действительно так. Курсы повышения квалификации, полный соцпакет, заграничный отпуск, медицинское обслуживание — всё это предлагает Газпром. Для нас с коллегами Газпром это в самом деле наша семья, которая нас объединяет, любит, заботится о нас в социальном, финансовом и культурном плане».

Тот факт, что газовый гигант вырос в экспортного монополиста и используется в качестве политического инструмента, не играет никакой роли для семьи Газпрома.

26-летний Артемий уже 5 лет работает инженером-электриком и курсирует между Тюменью и промыслом в Заполярном. Строго расписанная жизнь в Заполярье нравится отцу двоих детей. Вместо того, чтобы жаловаться на холод и темноту, он дорожит теплом и дружеской атмосферой, которая даёт ему защиту и уверенность.

«Ещё студентом я не раз бывал на практике, работал на различных предприятиях, накапливал опыт, поэтому мне есть с чем сравнивать. Здесь мне понравилось больше всего. Работа здесь интересней, чем где-либо — это лучшее рабочее место для меня. Мы здесь, правда, на краю земли, но зато у нас всё есть!»

Для «микроначальника», как называет себя Артемий, на газовых разработках Газпрома всё идёт как надо, но он хочет, чтобы было ещё лучше. На вопрос о том, что бы он изменил если бы мог, он отвечает прагматично.

«Газпром относительно консервативная компания, и революционные изменения в ней, на мой взгляд, не уместны. Достаточно, если мы примем во внимание новые стандарты в газовой добыче и организуем современные условия труда, если мы реализуем новые технологии и требования по сохранению экологии. Я хотел бы поработать тут подольше и оставить свой малый след в этом огромном предприятии и здесь, на Севере. Как люди, которые всё здесь построили. Они были удивительно мужественными, волевыми и терпеливыми. Я хочу хоть немного быть похожим на них. Но это нелегко!»

Главное место встреч в посёлке — спортивный и культурный центр. Огромное здание было построено в 2011 году. В 25-метровом бассейне можно плавать по своей дорожке с видом на белый полярный пейзаж. В футбольном и волейбольном зале проводятся турниры между разными отделами. В сауне, за игрой в настольный теннис, биллиард или дартс предоставляется возможность для дружеских встреч. Создаётся впечатление, что на 66-й широте всё-таки удалось перехитрить природу и суровый климат. Но и здесь не всё получается планировать. Бег на лыжах — новейший аттракцион для любителей зимних видов спорта. В прошлом году лыжная трасса была открыта только в апреле, потому что температура не поднималась выше минус 25 градусов. При таком морозе даже самым закалённым не разрешено выходить на лыжню, это может быть опасно для здоровья.

«Конечно, при занятиях спортом, здоровье наших людей стоит на первом месте. Тренировки должны способствовать укреплению организма. Ведь здесь трудно приспособиться: смена биоритма, удалённость от дома, дневная и ночная смена. Но спорт помогает легче переносить большие нагрузки и спокойно отработать смену без глубоких психических и эмоциональных переживаний».

Так рассказывают Борис и Костя, одни из многочисленных тренеров и спортивных врачей посёлка. Если же всё-таки работник заболевает, то о нем заботится целая армия врачей. Больница в Новозаполярном оборудована не хуже, чем обычная районная клиника где-нибудь в западной Европе.

Для тех, кто ищет просто спокойное место после окончания смены, разбит зимний сад. Здесь растут сотни белых и розовых орхидей, бугенвиллии, цветут миндальные деревца, маленькие лимоны и мандарины зреют на хрупких деревьях. В воздухе чувствуются испарения почвы, а в центре этого субтропического великолепия журчит ручей: лягушки и неуклюжие черепахи резвятся в воде. Идеальный мир Газпрома в ледяной пустыне.

«Девять месяцев в году зима. Не хватает зелени и солнца. Тогда ты приходишь сюда: сад, цветут растения и стоит такой аромат! От этого поднимается настроение и становится легко не сердце».

Сад восхищает не только садовников — в этой зелёной полярной идиллии очень часто можно встретить Кристину. Она приехала сюда не только за «длинным рублём» — прежде всего её привело в Заполярье любопытство.

«Я непременно хотела сюда приехать, хотела почувствовать — как это, когда 24 часа в сутки светит солнце, увидеть северное сияние, ненецкие чумы и северных оленей. Первое время я была в таком восторге, что не могла даже спать».

23-летняя Кристина приехала из столицы Мордовии Саранска. Кристина входит в команду из девяти человек, которые готовят культурную программу и тем самым вносят разнообразие в полярную жизнь. Здесь есть хор, театральная и танцевальная студии, киноклуб. Для представлений используется большой зал на 230 мест, оснащённый новейшей световой и звуковой аппаратурой. Кристина делает наброски и оформляет декорации и костюмы для представлений. Она отвечает за оформление дискотек, где каждую субботу стоит пыль столбом. С помощью заработанных здесь денег, Кристина оплачивает заочное обучение на учителя по изобразительному искусству.

Эта девушка не очень-то вписывается в суровый полярный пейзаж: тоненькая, лёгкая, как пёрышко, она и на работе носит джинсы с клетчатой мужской рубашкой. Два года назад она приехала в Новозаполярный, встретила здесь много интересных людей. Строгий распорядок жизни даётся ей легко.

«Здесь установлен строгий режим дня. Запрещены ночные прогулки, после 22:00 часов не разрешается выходить из дома. Только, что означает „не разрешается" — это не рекомендуется выходить из дома. Может быть, это и справедливо, и это хорошие правила, при таком экстремальном климате, но только, что же делать, если душа поёт!»

Для Лёши карьера в Газпроме была очевидна. Как и многие его коллеги, он выходец из династии газовиков. Его сестра и родители уже работали в Заполярном. Будучи двадцатиоднолетним, Лёша заступил на свою вахту, но прежде он попробовал себя в военной авиации. Теперь уже семь лет, как он принят в огромный концерн на работу слесарем.

«Я прослужил три года, причиной поменять работу была, как и у большинства, финансовая сторона вопроса. Условия здесь хорошие, работа интересная. Что можно было бы улучшить? Влияние профсоюза могло бы быть больше. И ещё больше оклад! Это везде животрепещущий вопрос».

15 лет назад, после первоначальной антипрофсоюзной кампании, был основан связанный с концерном Газпром Профсоюз. Как и более 80 процентов сотрудников Газпрома, Лёша является членом профсоюза. Собственно говоря, эта цифра просто фантастическая для представителя прав трудящихся. Тем не менее, профсоюз Газпрома не пользуется имеющейся у него возможностью, чтобы утвердиться как современная, мощная организация, призванная решать проблемы и удовлетворять нужды сотрудников. Как и другие связанные с концерном профсоюзы, он отказывается от радикальных мероприятий и настроен на дружественные отношения с работодателем, который, в свою очередь, поддерживает профсоюз морально и финансово.

Для большинства самое тяжелое в жизни и работе на Севере — не постоянные холода и темнота или строгий ежедневный распорядок, а долгая разлука с семьёй и друзьями. Даже если благодаря скайпу, фейсбуку и твиттеру любимые кажутся ближе, тоска по родным и близким не ослабевает.

«Самое трудное, что любимая жена не со мной! Я познакомился с ней здесь, это был вахтовый роман, большая любовь».

Как и Лёша, Артемий тоже скучает по своей семье. Он ждёт не дождётся встречи. Особенно окончания этой смены молодой отец ждёт с нетерпением. Помахать рукой своему новорождённому сыну он смог только в веб-камеру. Он возьмёт на руки своего богатыря, как Артемий его уже называет, только через несколько дней.

«Незадолго до отъезда домой, находишься в состоянии лёгкой эйфории от радости, что ты отработал смену с хорошим результатом и конечно, от скорой встречи с любимыми. Постоянно растёт желание увидеть родных и близких».

После недель интенсивного труда, путь газовиков лежит наконец-то домой, для многих на Большую землю. Они отдыхают от четырёх до шести недель в мягком климате, в кругу семьи. Потом опять прощание, и опять их ждет дорога к Полярному кругу, на очередную трудовую смену.

Эдуард Кондратьев со своей женой Леной много лет ведут совместную жизнь в ритме вахтового режима его работы. Эдуард курсирует между Новым Уренгоем и рабочим посёлком Новозаполярным уже 12 лет. Частые разлуки с семьёй даются ему всё ещё нелегко, даже несмотря на то, что он очень любит свою работу в заснеженной пустыне.

«Очень тяжело, когда рядом нет дорогих тебе людей. Печально, что ты не принимаешь участие в развитии своего ребёнка, не занимаешься его воспитанием, не помогаешь делать уроки. Это горько и больно сознавать».

Пока Эдуард работает на месторождении, Лена вместе с младшей дочерью Катей живёт в Новом Уренгое — на самом деле не так уж далеко от места работы её мужа, и всё-таки в недосягаемом отдалении от него. За все годы Лена ни разу не навещала мужа на его рабочем месте.

Как и многие здесь, семья Кондратьевых живёт в собственной квартире в панельном доме, в одном из самых дорогих городов России. До перестройки экономической системы квартиры предоставлялись за умеренную квартплату. Позже появилась возможность выкупать квартиры в собственность, причем по довольно дорогой цене: квадратный метр жилья в Приполярье стоит примерно 1 500 евро.

Состояние жилых зданий в городе находится в резком контрасте с современными технологиями газовой отрасли. Снежные зимы оставили свои следы на обветшалых панельных домах с плохой теплоизоляцией. Темные, сырые и запущенные подъезды, поцарапанные и поломанные почтовые ящики на грязных стенах при входе. Ничейная земля, за которую никто не несёт ответственности.

За тяжёлой металлической дверью — уютный рай Кондратьевых. Они превратили стандартную трёхкомнатную квартиру в современный светлый дом, оснащённый по лучшим стандартам: телевизор с плоским экраном, стереоустановка, компьютер, плита, посудомоечная машина и джакузи в ванной. Трудно поверить, но разница температур снаружи и внутри нередко достигает семидесяти градусов. Центральное газовое отопление в квартирах поддерживает температуру на уровне комфортных 25-ти градусов и это по фиксированной цене! Для регулирования температуры открывается окно. Экономное обращение с природными запасами и энергией в газовой столице не стоит на первом месте.

«Мы привыкли к Новому Уренгою. Если мы едем в отпуск, через некоторое время нас тянет домой. Этот город — мой дом, хотя я и не здесь родилась. Мой отец уехал на работу на север, устроился здесь и перевёз семью. Когда я сюда приехала, меня удивило, что здесь так много молодёжи и детей. Все были какими-то особенными, открытыми и сердечными».

Лена Кондратьева хорошо помнит, как она молодой девушкой переехала в Новый Уренгой из Кишинёва, расположенного теперь в Молдавии, со всей своей семьёй. О том, что люди здесь особенные, о дружелюбном «северном человеке» и северянах часто слышишь в Приполярье.

«Люди на Большой земле живут уютней: тепло, вино, цветы и море. Там люди другие. У нас же своё собственное воспитание, северное. Здесь люди ближе друг другу и живут дружнее».

Эдуард поясняет, что северянин открыт, всегда готов помочь и умеет дружить. О причине таких особенностей можно только догадываться. Возможно люди здесь такие потому, что на Крайнем Севере очень трудно выжить в одиночку.

Когда Катя, несмотря на лютый мороз, выходит на улицу, она идёт в Гудзон. Торговый центр Гудзон — двухэтажное стеклянное строение, один из нескольких торговых центров Нового Уренгоя. Здесь выстроились в ряд огромные магазины электроники, игрушек, филиалы известных модных и парфюмерных брендов, как и во многих крупных европейских городах. Супермаркет предлагает покупателям впечатляющий ассортимент продуктов: от свежей пасты до детского лакомства «Киндерсюрприз», от кефира до французского коньяка, от папайи и киви до биологически чистых продуктов.

Жители города пользуются разнообразными возможностями для совершения покупок, но всё же здесь довольно спокойно. В кафе и ресторанах много свободных мест, мало кто рассматривает витрины магазинов. Здесь нет музыкантов, и, конечно, никаких бездомных и пьяных. Не видно и молодёжи, которая проводила бы здесь свободное время. Это удивляет, хотя чего ожидать от местности, где низкие температуры девять месяцев в году не позволяют находиться на свежем воздухе, гулять по бульварам, полежать в парке или на берегу реки. Детские площадки тоже занесены снегом. На этом фоне даже помещения под крышей торгового центра становятся заманчивым местом встреч.

Те, кто любит петь, танцевать, посещать театр или заниматься спортом, могут проводить свободное время в культурно-спортивном комплексе «Газовик», который находится под управлением отдела культуры Газпром Добыча Уренгой. Здесь каждый найдёт что-нибудь себе по душе. Волейбольная команда «Факел», спонсируемая Газпромом, проводит здесь свои домашние игры. Во время больших праздников, концертов и представлений все места в зале заняты. Кто приедет в газовую столицу развлекать жителей, решает Газпром. Одна из участниц театральной труппы сожалеет о том, что развлекательные программы строго регламентированы. Каждый проект или гастроли должны быть утверждены отделом культуры Газпрома.

Создаётся впечатление, что в торговом центре, культурно-спортивном комплексе и на других площадках для проведения досуга всё управляется слишком уж организованно. Возможно, только в собственных четырёх стенах люди могут самостоятельно наладить свою жизнь, оставив все правила газового концерна снаружи. В любом случае, очень многие жители Нового Уренгоя называют самым любимым местом в городе свой собственный дом.

«Какое моё любимое место в Новом Уренгое? Конечно же, мой дом! В детстве квартира родителей была для меня самым лучшим местом на свете, теперь у меня есть своё собственное уютное гнездо!»

Неважно, проводят ли жители города свободное время с семьёй и друзьями, или просто наслаждаются отдыхом дома — жизнь Нового Уренгоя проходит под знаком работы, поэтому мест для досуга здесь не так уж много. Это касается и молодых жителей: уже от подростков требуются целеустремлённость и усердие.

Газовая промышленность оказывает влияние на многие области жизни, образование — одна из них. Особенно много Газпром инвестирует в подготовку молодых специалистов. В северной части города расположен техникум газовой промышленности, который основал и финансирует Газпром. Около 1 000 учеников обучаются здесь в течение четырёх лет, по таким специальностям, как техник газодобычи, экономист и бухгалтер. Обязательной частью учебного плана является практика в крупнейшем газовом концерне. Пресс-секретарь Сергей Чернецкий объяснил, что, наряду с наилучшими профессиональными знаниями, здесь ценятся командный дух, способность к адаптации, стрессоустойчивость, ответственность и честность.

«Мы не благотворительная организация, мы выбираем лучших из лучших. Но это не значит, что мы собираем только сливки: мы инвестируем много времени и сил, чтобы привлечь и удержать сотрудников. Как раз в последнее время многие… нет, не многие, а некоторые сотрудники перешли в независимые предприятия, потому что они там, наверно, больше зарабатывают».

Газпром регулярно организует информационные мероприятия в крупнейших технических университетах страны: в Уфе, Казани, Краснодаре, Тюмени, Москве или Санкт-Петербурге, приглашая всех заинтересованных студентов на собеседование в газовую столицу, чтобы привлечь их перспективой получить надёжную и хорошо оплачиваемую работу.

Однако воспитание рабочей смены начинается еще в школе. Концерн Газпром старается поощрять особенно одарённых школьников, чтобы уже в молодые годы завоевать их в качестве своих будущих сотрудников.

16-летний Дима, фанат немецкой рок-музыки, учится в спонсируемом Газпромом классе в городской гимназии Нового Уренгоя. Этот класс был создан только в прошлом году. Классная комната оформлена в цветах концерна и оборудована современнейшей техникой, на интерактивной доске красуется факел-логотип. Здесь готовят к возможной работе в компании лучших из лучших.

Когда температура опускается ниже сорока градусов, ученики освобождаются от занятий в школе и могут получить домашнее задание по интернету. Одним щелчком мышки школьники могут отослать сделанные уроки в школу. Как и все ученики, Дима и его одноклассники радуются, когда здесь, в Приполярье, отменяются уроки. В такие дни, а они здесь нередки, подростки могут выспаться. В общем, совершенно нормальные школьники — разве что уже в шестнадцатилетнем возрасте они точно знают, кем хотят стать и почему.

«Если ты принят в класс Газпрома, ты получишь больше знаний, потому что в этом классе специалисты читают нам лекции, которые не услышишь в других. Кроме того, это большой шанс попасть в будущем на работу в Газпром. Это великолепная перспектива! Надёжный, высокий заработок. Перед тобой открывается большое будущее».

Класс Газпрома стоит более 50 000 евро в год, такие классы в недалёком будущем должны быть открыты по всей России, чтобы воспитывать остро необходимую рабочую смену. Но Газпром ценится высоко не только как работодатель для специалистов газовой промышленности. Почти каждый житель Нового Уренгоя не против получить рабочее место в Газпроме.

«Ты можешь с гордостью сказать, что ты работаешь в Газпроме».

Татьяна Борисовна говорит от имени коллектива детского сада. Среди многочисленных детских садов города, Газпром содержит восемь собственных, два из которых являются специальными профильными «Профилакториями». Это «Белоснежка» на юге и «Морозко» на севере города. Ребёнок должен добираться до своего детского сада не более пары минут. Город делает много для того, чтобы защитить своих детей в суровом климате и восполнить недостаток движения на свежем воздухе: детские сады располагают спортивными залами и плавательными бассейнами, леса и поля в мини версиях представлены зимними садами, притом в каждом детском саду города. Но Газпром на этом не останавливается.

В «Морозко», который был признан лучшим детским садом России, 72 человека — воспитатели, повара и работники кухни, ЛОР-врачи и педиатры, логопеды и физиотерапевты — заботятся о благополучии 220 детей.

«Медицинское обследование наших детей очень важно для нас. Северный климат негативно влияет на здоровье детей и взрослых. Здесь же экстремальные условия».

Офтальмолог проверяет зрение и подбирает очки, логопед корректирует речь, массажистки разминают напряжённые мышцы у полуторагодовалых детей. После сауны малышам накрывают столы и подают чай. Потом они идут в игровые комнаты, забитые до потолка игрушками. И, как вишенка на торте: то, что делает этот детский сад самым лучшим — соляная комната. В затемнённом помещении, стены и потолок которого напоминают пещеру, в шапках и варежках дети лежат в кроватках, смотрят мультфильмы и дышат воздухом, насыщенным солью и другими веществами, которые предупреждают воспаление лёгких. После процедуры предлагается пенистый напиток.

«Здесь, на Севере, мы боремся с недостатком кислорода. Поэтому наши дети получают кислородный коктейль, чтобы восполнить этот недостаток».

Добро пожаловать на «космический корабль Морозко»! О необходимости кислородного напитка можно конечно поспорить, или просто поинтересоваться научными данными. Как Российские, так и немецкие, эксперты утверждают, что содержание кислорода в воздухе на Полярном Круге не ниже, чем где-либо на земле, но миф о недостатке кислорода на Крайнем Севере всё-таки прижился.

«Моя армия сильная, сильная! Моя армия смелая, смелая! Моя армия гордая, гордая!», — разносятся трелли высокого детского голоса из динамиков по коридорам «Морозко» в честь предстоящего праздника Дня защитника Отечества. И в заключение гимн, льющийся из уст ребёнка, возвращает посетителя с космической орбиты, якобы бедной кислородом, назад, в атмосферу вполне нормального российского детского сада, где даже самые маленькие должны учиться уважать армию и родину любить.

Много средств вкладывается в развитие Нового Уренгоя и в будущее его жителей. Какими бы огромными ни были планы и усилия, жизнеспособность города полностью зависит от предприятий по добыче сырья. Однако в газовой столице этот факт не вызывает беспокойства. Истощённые газовые месторождения и сокращающиеся ресурсы не являются проблемой, Новый Уренгой останется важным форпостом Газпрома.

«Понятно, что год за годом газа будет добываться меньше. На некоторых месторождениях объём добычи находится на самом пике, это положение продержится, возможно, ещё пять — шесть лет. Потом добыча сократится и будут разрабатываться новые месторождения дальше на севере, но там не планируется строить новые города, только небольшие посёлки для вахтовиков. Новый Уренгой останется плацдармом».

Разработка газовых месторождений наносит ущерб ненцам, кочевникам-оленеводам, охотникам и рыболовам, которые живут в автономном Ямало-Ненецком округе и дали ему имя. Каждое газодобывающее предприятие наносит вред природе, добыча полезных ископаемых изначально плохо сказывается на окружающей среде и коренном населении.

Это хорошо известно пресс-секретарю Сергею Чернецкому. Он многословно подчёркивает хорошие отношения между ненцами и газовым гигантом, указывает на мероприятия, посредством которых Газпром пытается возместить урон от отобранных у коренного населения пастбищ:

Газпром спонсирует строительство посёлков для кочевников на севере региона, Газпром построил интернат и оплачивает бесплатное образование для подростков. Здесь с удовольствием совместно празднуются традиционные праздники кочевников — День оленевода или День рыбака. Выглядит почти как идиллия, но на самом деле это не так. За благожелательностью стоят экономические интересы. Чтобы сохранить прибыли от газодобычи, промышленность будет проникать во все более отдаленные районы и даже на дно Северного Ледовитого океана, где предполагаются большие запасы природного газа.

Всё больше и больше людей будут ездить на Север, чтобы обслуживать газовую индустрию и добывать полезные ископаемые, на которые есть устойчивый спрос. Но не только новые месторождения создают много рабочих мест, Новый Уренгой так же привлекает хорошо оплачиваемой работой, будь то врач или учитель, строитель или официантка — в газовой столице каждому найдётся работа. Управление архитектуры и строительства должно не только обеспечивать хороший уровень жизни для жителей, но и постоянно его повышать. Здесь все время ведётся строительство и модернизация, шаг за шагом субарктический ландшафт превращается в городской.

«Перед нами стоит трудная задача: построить новые дома для людей, которые живут в ветхих жилищах. Эта задача очень важная и её надо быстро решить. Старые здания были построены быстро, но тогда было не до красоты. Сегодня мы пытаемся придать новым городским районам особое лицо, чтобы они не выглядели скучными. Мы занимаемся озеленением, прокладываем бульвары и разбиваем парки. И это всё делается для обеспечения высокого качества жизни в городе».

На юге, где ещё недавно стояли одноэтажные деревянные дома и бараки, вырос новый жилой район «Тундра». Он особо не отличается от районов, построенных в советские времена. Панельные пяти- и девятиэтажки повернуты лицом к лицу вокруг большого внутреннего двора. Во дворе, в пяти минутах ходьбы, расположены детский сад и школа. Скоро 1 400 семей смогут заселиться в новые квартиры. Разработчик проекта привлекает покупателей новыми строительными технологиями, эффективной теплоизоляцией и большой парковкой. Фасады, состоящие из готовых бетонных блоков, облицованы бежевыми и коричневыми плитами и украшены красными навесами, башенками и фронтонами.

Новое веяние — планировка района с частными домами. Мода на собственный дом с садом, даже если этот сад будет использоваться ежегодно только короткое время, теперь дошла и до Полярного Круга.

«В последние годы ситуация несколько изменилась. Возрос спрос на частные дома. Причина в том, что люди остаются здесь дольше, чем предполагали первоначально».

На градостроителей возложена новая задача: как в южной части города, так и в северной разработать план по постройке районов с частными домами. Трудно себе представить, что в будущем в Приполярье вырастут бунгало и виллы, каждый дом — крепость в снежной пустыне — будет снабжаться теплом, водой и электроэнергией. Но нет никаких сомнений, что и это возможно в Газпром Сити.

Хотя жители живут в этом приполярном городе не пару лет, а целыми десятилетиями, навечно оставаться на Крайнем Севере никто не хочет. Самое позднее после выхода на пенсию, люди переезжают на землю, на Большую землю. Этот город в Приполярье всё-таки не предназначен для пожилых людей.

После двадцати лет рабочего стажа на крайнем севере, женщины могут в 50 лет выйти на заслуженную пенсию, мужчины должны отработать на 5 лет дольше. При особенно суровых условиях труда обязательный рабочий стаж сокращается на несколько лет.

«Ты делаешь свою работу добросовестно, на высоком уровне. И ты уезжаешь отсюда с высоко поднятой головой. Без сомнения, ты заслужил всё, что хотел. Ты получил всё: признание, почетные грамоты, медали. В общем, если ты усердно трудишься, ты можешь, выйдя на пенсию, жить без забот».

Большинство мечтает о дальнейшей жизни после выхода на пенсию, после отъезда из этого города. Газпром помогает своим работникам осуществить эти мечты. Концерн предлагает программу долгосрочного финансирования покупки жилья «в России». Работники выплачивают только малую часть. Они погружаются в планирование будущего дома. Так, долгими зимними месяцами, на многих кухнях Нового Уренгоя люди продумывают детали, разрабатывают конкретные планы. Сотрудники самой крупной газодобывающей компании не отрываются от жизни в своих мечтах, а твёрдо стоят обеими ногами на родной земле.

«Есть ли у меня планы о том, что я буду делать на пенсии? Самое главное — построить дом, виллу, обязательно двухэтажную, чтобы мои дети и внуки в любое время могли меня навестить и чтоб для каждого был свой уголок. У меня будет одна большая собака в доме, вторая будет сторожевая, во дворе. Да, у нас будет две собаки, кошка и огромный аквариум. Я хочу разбить сад с цветами, кустарником, ягодами — и чтобы никакого картофельного поля! Сад, где можно поставить стол со стульями, самовар. Пить чай по вечерам, вокруг бегают дети, если жарко, то можно поплавать в бассейне. И где-нибудь стоит гриль и вся семья собирается вместе. Там должно быть так хорошо, что все всегда будут рады возвращаться домой».

In early February, we take a Russian S7 Airlines plane from Moscow to Novy Urengoy, Russia's gas capital in Western Siberia. The flight is booked up to the very last seat. There are hardly any older passengers on board, and the young ones are definitely not equipped for a polar expedition. It is only the two of us that are sweating in our thick down jackets and winter boots. The flight takes nearly three-and-a-half hours; we fly over an endless desert of snow almost the entire time. Every now and then, a small settlement or the glow of a gas flare appears in the dawn.

Without Gulnaz Kolokolova, a friendly Gazprom employee, and without the *propusk*, the permit that identifies us as guests of the gas extracting company Gazprom and that opens many doors, our journey would have come to its end at passport control. The city is closed to foreigners. You need a special permit from the energy company in order to visit it. We made countless requests to Gazprom, we inquired again and again, until the head office in Moscow finally gave the go-ahead.

What was the motivation for a journey to this city in the Arctic Circle, which offers not so much attractions as large industrial facilities and where the weather is far from pleasant?

The mutual interdependence of Western Europe and Russia resulting from imports and exports of natural gas and the weighty position of Gazprom receive regular attention in politics and the media. The emphasis is usually on the consequences this dependence has for the consumers at the European end of the gas pipeline. However, the circumstances of the gas production and the living conditions of the people at the source in Western Siberia are barely ever discussed.

How do the people of Novy Urengoy live, here in this city that is completely dependent on natural gas resources and where life is dictated by the big corporation?

In the parking lot in front of the airport, a digital display shows 45 degrees below zero. One's glasses ice over in seconds, and it hurts to breathe. A driver from Gazprom is already expecting us and takes us to the Hotel 'North Star'. In the following ten days, we want to get to know the company town and experience as much as possible of its everyday life.

Beyond the Big Earth

VOICES FROM A CITY IN THE POLAR CIRCLE

'There is one sole reason for the existence of the city of Novy Urengoy: the Urengoy gas field. Without the presence of these natural resources there would be no city. Our city is often called "the natural gas capital" or simply Gazprom City.'

It has been almost 50 years since the Urengoy gas field was discovered in Western Siberia. It is one of the biggest gas fields in the world. The systematic development of the natural gas industry began here, far from any populated areas, in the swampy lakeland of the Sub-arctic tundra.

To contribute to this ambitious venture, many volunteered to move to the hostile region, where the temperatures fall below freezing point between September and May and the thermometer often drops to more than 50 degrees below zero. Transportation routes were built, production facilities were set up, hundreds of kilometres of pipeline were laid, and little by little a small settlement for workers grew into the northern city of Novy Urengoy.

Eduard Kondratyev was eight years old when, in the mid-1970s, his parents and their three children moved from southern Russia to the polar circle to work on the development of the natural gas industry, and earn good money while doing so. Thousands of other people did the same.

'I remember exactly how it was at that time. These are special memories that will stay with me my entire life. They are so strong that I will probably never leave. That is the unique spirit of the North! In the first years, we lived in so-called "barrels", similar to propped-up waggons. Usually, two or even three families lived on about 15 square metres. In the morning, our parents went to work, and the children were left alone with toys cobbled together from tins. Those are truly lasting impressions.'

A narrow strip of land, nearly eleven kilometres long and situated on the southern end of the Urengoy gas field, was selected as the location for the city of the gas field workers. It is enclosed by two tributaries of the River Pur and surrounded by thousands and thousands of lakes and ponds, which, in the winter, disappear under a thick cover of snow. A sign with the name of the town was driven into the ground beside the makeshift shelters of the workers. Eduard has witnessed how the sparse lodgings and wooden huts made way for well-constructed living modules. He was there when streets and residential quarters were built and when supply lines were dug into the permafrost soil to supply the residents with light and heat.

The plans for the city were quickly outlined on the drawing board in accordance with the rules of socialist urban planning. Standardised housing units, grouped around a court-yard with a public building – usually a school or a kindergarten –, were pulled up along the city's main artery. The construction combine No. 3 in Leningrad produced the pre-fabricated concrete elements for the residential buildings: the *plattenbau* design 1-LG-600. The 600-series is often called 'the ship', as the long horizontal lines of windows resemble an ocean liner.

All buildings are alike, only the façades, painted in different colours, provide orientation. Several housing blocks make up the various neighbourhoods, the so-called microrayons. They have fine-sounding names, being dedicated to the 'optimists' and 'enthusiasts', the 'builders of the roads' – or, more simply, to the 'polar landscape' and 'sunshine'. The hospital, the administration buildings, and the leisure facilities are situated between the residential areas. There is no real city centre. When living space became sparse, the city spread across the river. The northern city district Severka was built, with neighbourhoods bearing the names 'Friendship', 'Peace', 'Soviet', and 'Anniversary'.

Today, Novy Urengoy is a prosperous metropolis with more than 110,000 inhabitants. Three quarters of all Russian natural gas is produced in the area, in a complex system of gas processing plants that have been built and are controlled by the Gazprom group. The vast majority of the inhabitants of the city works in the gas industry, for Gazprom or one of its countless subsidiaries or partner companies.

Eduard, too, can look back on a successful career with Gazprom. Now 44 years old, he has assumed various roles in the course of the years. Today, he is chief engineer at Gazprom Dobycha Yamburg. There have been tempting offers from the Gazprom headquarters in Moscow to work in the capital. But he has remained in Novy Urengoy because of his passion for the North. It is here that he met his wife Lena and that he has raised his children Yuri, Alexandra, and Katya. In his spare time, he enjoys nature, taking walks to spot reindeer, ptarmigans and white Arctic foxes – not to hunt them, but because he likes to watch them and take pictures. Or he goes fishing in one of the crystal-clear rivers of Western Siberia.

'You just have to look out of the window to see what wonders are happening. Everything is magnificent – the nature, the space, the vast expanse… they are unbelievable. The production and the technology are immense. There are so many treasures hidden deep underground. The work is endless here, too.'

To this day, many, mostly young, Russians are drawn to the North by the promise of making good money in the company town. A job in the gas industry stands for a secure and – by Russian standards – high income. For this, they put up with living in one of the most isolated areas on earth, which is dominated entirely by the extractive industry.

'When Novy Urengoy was founded, there was a so-called city-forming enterprise, today the Gazprom Corporation, which set up the essential infrastructure, for example residential buildings, streets, schools, and kindergartens. Today, this responsibility is in our hands.'

These hands are Yevgeny Voroshilov's. He is the chief urban planner of Novy Urengoy. Three years ago, the architect, who was born in the Crimea, moved to the Arctic Circle with his wife and two children so he could take up this position. Since 2006, the Urban Planning Department has been responsible for urban development and all building projects. Before, all this had been the remit of Gazprom.

In the opinion of the architect, on the whole Novy Urengoy functions just like any other city – it's just that it's situated north of the polar circle. There is a power station, an incineration facility and a sewage plant. Food is mainly sourced from outside suppliers, though some is produced in the city. There is a bread factory and one for meat products, as well as a large greenhouse. Fresh milk is no longer produced in the gas capital – the dairy cows were resettled from the North for economic reasons. In their free time, people go to the cinema, visit the Natural Gas Museum, or go bowling in the 'Snowy Owl'; they go see a show in the

Palace of Culture or watch a match in one of the huge sports halls. There is an Orthodox church and a mosque. Many nationalities came to live in the city in Soviet times: Russians, Belarusians, Ukrainians, Tartars, Kumyks, Azerbaijani, Bashkirs, and Chechens.

'Novy Urengoy is a city for gas field workers. It was built with great ambition by volunteers. Many have helped with the construction work or have otherwise made a contribution to the building of the city, and they have often become friends. There is a very special spirit present here that makes the hard conditions bearable. It is a city in which architecture is mainly about functionality. The whole city is a memorial in honour of labour and of those who have built it and developed the gas fields.'

Since the development of the Urengoy gas field, 6.5 trillion cubic metres of gas have been produced – a top performance, which earned the area an entry in the Guinness Book of World Records. Never before has such a gigantic quantity of natural gas been extracted from a single deposit – and the Urengoy gas field is not the only one to have been discovered and developed in this veritable gas eldorado. The Yamburg gas field was tapped in 1986, the Zapolyarnoye field in 2001; the Yuzhno-Russkoye and Beregovoye fields were connected to the grid in 2007, and lastly, in 2012, the Samburgskoye field was opened. It takes more than mere statistics or press releases to record such a success story.

Gazprom, Russian warrior!
Planet Gazprom
Onwards, Gazprom! Onwards, Gazprom!

These are the names of the anthems that glorify the world's biggest energy company in word and sound. They are reminiscent of the Soviet era's patriotic workers' songs.

Until 1992, Gazprom was subordinated to the Ministry of Oil and Gas Industry. Since then it has been a public joint-stock company. The state owns 50 percent plus one of the company shares and has the majority of seats on the supervisory board. With its roughly 459,000 employees, Gazprom is one of the largest employers in the country and bolsters the Russian national budget with billions. It is the most relevant provider of foreign exchange for Russia and the most important energy supplier for many countries in Central Europe that are dependent on the natural gas of Western Siberia.

Since the gas resources that are being newly developed are increasingly distant from populated areas, Novy Urengoy has now taken over the function of a bridgehead: It's where the workforces arrive for a first stop before continuing their journey to the Arctic gas fields. Intermittently, over 20,000 shift workers work on the gas fields around Novy Urengoy. Many commute from distant regions of Russia, others directly from the gas capital. Gazprom Dobycha Yamburg and Gazprom Dobycha Urengoy have their head offices in the city. From here they manage production, transport and distribution of the gas within Russia and onwards to foreign countries and co-ordinate the legions of employees, which are essential for the production of natural gas.

Buses with workers depart the city from the airport towards Zapolyarnoye. This natural gas field is situated 220 kilometres northeast of Novy Urengoy. Road guards are stationed at the city boundary. In this area of strategic importance, everybody that leaves the city is controlled, not just visitors from abroad. If the outdoor temperature drops below minus 45 degrees, the buses have to drive in convoys for safety reasons. The routes are well developed, the landscape is covered in deep snow. You can just about make out the River Pur, which is meandering through the lowlands. Along the riverside grow birch trees, larches, arolla pines, and spruces. After a short drive, the landscape changes entirely: it is now a vast and seemingly boundless desert of snow. Nothing obstructs the view – no settlements, no hills or forests, you only see the horizon. Only the steel pylons, covered in ice, and occasional gas flares – the Gazprom symbol – provide a diversion in these monotonous surroundings.

The surreal effect of the icy landscape is complete when, at very low temperatures and a certain angle of the sun, colourful light columns shine straight up into the sky. What's very real, however, are the many lorries, buses, and SUVs that drive on this frosty route. It is impossible to imagine that, in the short snow-free period between June and August, plants can flourish here, the tundra blossoms, mushrooms pop out of the ground, and the berry bushes bloom and later will bear fruit. The summer lasts just 35 days.

Amidst this endless expanse of snow, 60 kilometres north of the Arctic Circle, lies UKPG-2S, one of Zapolyarnoye's five gas treatment units. One is only permitted to enter the fenced-in premises after another check of the identification documents. The industrial complex consists of several hangars and a kilometre-long pipe system. Around the gas processing plant, the natural gas streams out to the surface from a depth of 3,000 metres, arriving through big, jacked-up pipes in a hall that is almost devoid of humans. No voices are heard, only the monotonous whistling and hissing of the machinery. A tangle of thick and thin colourful pipes, nozzles, tanks, and measuring devices that check quantity, density, pressure, and temperature level. There's no sweat here, no grease, no machine oil – only high-tech at an extraordinary level.

'Here, we extract 130 billion cubic metres of natural gas annually. That is more than the annual gas consumption of Germany. The gas is of high quality and consists of 98.8 percent methane. The remnants of propane, butane, and nitrogen are minimal. And we don't get much water, either – only two-hundred grams per thousand cubic metres of extracted gas.'

Azad Gumerov, Deputy Head of the plant, has worked on the Western Siberian gas fields for years. He tells of the extraordinary output of gas with some pride; he has all the relevant figures and data to hand immediately.

You rarely see one of the technicians with their white helmets and blue jackets, emblazoned with the Gazprom logo, on the premises. Gone are the days at the end of the last century when tons of sand were heaped onto the marshy tundra; gone is the time when huge drilling heads penetrated the ground to get to the gas layers and brought debris and mud up to the surface. Today, UKPG-2S is an almost clinically clean facility. All operations are computer-controlled. Day and night, two dispatchers are monitoring each individual phase of the gas treatment process on huge screens. The data are forwarded to the control centre, known as the 'heart'. The staff members here aren't dressed in Gazprom workwear, they're wearing dark suits. If any irregularities occur in the intricate network, red indicators begin flashing. One of the screens indicates how much gas has been produced in the last two hours and compares this amount to the daily targets. The mood is relaxed. With one eye, the young men watch a hockey game on TV.

Before the gas leaves the production plant, an aromatic substance is added for safety reasons, because natural gas is colour- and odourless. Once compressed, cooled, and scented, it is sent off through the pipelines. During its long journey to the end consumer, once in every 100 kilometres it passes compressor stations that ensure it travels at the correct speed. The gas needs about seven to twelve days to travel from the gas fields in the Yamalo-Nenets Autonomous Okrug to Central Europe – a distance of almost 3,700 kilometres.

UKPG-2S never sleeps. From the executive floor to the technicians, everybody works according to the *vakhtovy metod*: day or night shifts of twelve hours, including Sundays and holidays, for one month; or nine hours per day for six days in a row, for six weeks. To put it simply:

'When we are working shifts, it's always Monday, every day is a Monday. But once we get home, it's always the weekend. That's how the schedule is!'

During work periods, 4,000 workers live in the settlement of Novozapolyarny that was built nearby the processing plants in 2001. Three-storeyed apartment buildings with pink-and-yellow façades are lined up alongside a generously laid-out boulevard. Cast-iron street lamps cast their dim glow onto the streets. The buildings are embellished with banners and billboards. Though Gazprom's blue has taken over from Soviet red, they are no less patriotic than those of a bygone era.

Energy: the lifeline of Russia!
Hurrah for the achievements of the gas field workers!
Glory be labour!
Zapolyarnoye – 130 billion cubic metres of gas per year!

The majority of workers live in two identical apartment complexes. You enter each building through a spacious entrance hall decorated with houseplants, fish tanks, a lounge area, flat-screen TVs, and numerous cash machines. From here you have access to the cafeteria, the billiard room, the sports hall, and the gym, or you can go directly to the sleeping quarters. The single and double rooms lie along endless corridors and are all furnished identically: kitchenette, shower room, bed, wardrobe, television set, bookshelf. The furnishing is not luxurious, but not overly cheap, either. Only a few details indicate whether it's a man or a woman living here. But in fact, people don't really live here, anyway: they only sleep here.

In the shift workers camp everything is strictly regulated. The workers must not leave the compound and are not allowed to receive friends or relatives. Curfew is at 10 pm. Drinking alcohol is strictly forbidden. Numerous inspectors, most of them female, ensure that the rules are observed.

The residential area comes to life only during shift change, in the morning and in the evening. Caretakers have swept the fresh snow from the stairs leading to the entrances. Engineers and technicians, canteen staff and watchmen rush to the blue Gazprom buses that take them to their workplace. Nobody walks longer distances than absolutely necessary at 50 degrees below zero. Apart from the sound of running engines coming from the buses, everything is very quiet. Even speaking is painful when it's this cold.

The winter is long; it lasts 284 days a year. The days in December and January are extremely short, the shortest day lasts just over one hour. But the *dlinny rubl*, the 'long rouble', lures thousands of young men and women to Gazprom's gas fields, despite the extreme conditions.

People like 33-year-old Ais, father of three children, who came to the Arctic Circle from the southern steppes of Kalmykia, close to the Caspian Sea. Ais works as a driver in the Novozapolyarny settlement. He's full of enthusiasm when he talks about his work.

'This job is prestigious and the salary is good – remarkably good, you hardly find that anywhere else. I have children, a boy and two girls… I must feed my family. And the employee benefits are fantastic: there are free trips to the Black Sea with a stay at a health resort, for the children, too, and bonuses!'

None of the Gazprom employees are willing to disclose exact figures regarding salary levels, and neither is the administrative centre in Novy Urengoy. But everyone that's interviewed confirms that the packages – salaries and benefits – are significantly higher than in the rest of Russia. Like all large companies around the world, Gazprom tries to keep its employees by offering high wages and bonuses. Apparently, this approach is working.

'The TV ads often say that Gazprom makes dreams come true. And that really is the case. Career advancement and training, generous employee benefits, vacations abroad, healthcare – Gazprom offers all that. For me and my colleagues Gazprom is really our family that unites us, loves us, cares for us – socially, financially, and culturally.'

The fact that the gas giant has a monopoly on gas exports and has moreover become a political tool is of little significance to the Gazprom family.

The 26-year-old electrical engineer Artemi from Tyumen has commuted to the Zapolyarnoye gas field for five years. A father of two children, he likes the stable, orderly life he leads in the polar circle. Rather than complaining about the cold and the darkness, he appreciates the warm and friendly atmosphere that lends him safety and protection.

'I already did various internships when I was still a student. I worked in several businesses and was able to gain practical experience, so I was in a good position to compare different options. This is where I liked it best. The work is more interesting than anywhere else. For me, it is the best place to work. We might be at the end of the world, but we want for nothing!'

All is going smoothly for the 'micro-boss', as Artemi calls himself, but his ambitions go even further. When asked what he would change if he could, his reply is pragmatic.

'Gazprom is a relatively conservative company and I don't believe revolutionary changes would be appropriate. It is sufficient when we comply with new standards of gas extraction and implement new ecological and technological requirements. I would like to work for Gazprom for a long time and make a small impression on this gigantic enterprise up here in the North. Like the men who have built up all this. I admire their courage, their determination, and their patience. I would like to be a little bit like them. But that requires a great deal of energy!'

The sports and cultural centre is the main meeting point of the Novozapolyarny settlement. The gigantic building was erected in 2011. In the 25-metre pool you can swim your laps with a view of the white polar landscape. Tournaments between the various departments of the company are held on indoor football pitches and volleyball courts. Sauna, table tennis, pool, and darts are just some of the activities on offer for social get-togethers. It would appear as if here, at a latitude of 66 degrees, the raw nature and extreme climate have successfully been outsmarted. So it is almost reassuring to hear that not all goes to plan. In the last year, a cross-country trail – the newest attraction for winter sports enthusiasts – could not be opened until April, because the temperatures didn't rise above minus 25 degrees before that. Below this temperature, not even the toughest sportspeople are allowed on the trail, as that would pose a serious health risk.

'With our sports programmes, we place the health and wellbeing of our people above everything else. Doing sports is meant to make them even fitter. Adapting to the conditions here is difficult: for instance, people's biorhythm changes, they're being so far away from home, they're working day and night. Sports helps to take the pressure off and to endure the hard shifts, mentally and physically, without suffering any significant lows.'

That is how Boris and Kostya, two of the many coaches and sport therapists at the settlement, explain the significance physical activity has here. If, despite all their efforts, one of the employees falls ill, a veritable army of physicians looks after the patient. Novozapolyarny's medical department is no worse than any standard regional hospital in Western Europe.

For those that are simply looking for a bit of peace and quiet after working hours, there is the winter garden. It beats everything else; it's the ultimate retreat. Here, white and pink orchids and bougainvilleas grow, almond trees blossom and small lemons and tangerines ripen on delicate trees. The soil is steaming. And there's the ripple of a tiny stream that flows right through this subtropical splendour north of the Arctic Circle. Frogs and turtles frolic in the water. Gazprom's little paradise in the polar desert.

'Nine months of winter! That makes people yearn for verdant nature and the feel of summer. So they come here: to a real garden. Flowers are blooming, and it's so fragrant – that lifts the spirits and makes you feel light and full of joy.'

It's not only the gardener who's raptured by the winter garden. Kristina, too, can frequently be found in this polar idyll. Besides the 'long rouble', it was mainly curiosity that brought her to the North.

'I wanted to come here so much. I wanted to know what it feels like when the sun is shining for 24 hours a day. I wanted to experience the aurora borealis, to see reindeers, and the tents of the Nenets. In the beginning, I was so excited that I couldn't sleep.'

The 23-year-old woman is from Saransk, the capital of Mordovia. Kristina is part of the team of nine that is responsible for bringing variety and distraction to everyday life in the polar circle by means of a cultural programme. There is a choir, a theatre and dance group, and a film club. A large hall with 230 seats and state-of-the-art lighting and sound technology is available for events. Kristina designs and makes costumes and stage sets for the shows. She decorates the disco where all hell breaks loose every Saturday. She uses the money she earns for financing her distance learning course in art pedagogy.

Kristina doesn't really seem to fit into this harsh polar landscape. She is very slight and looks as light as a feather. Even when working, she wears jeans and a plaid shirt. She came to Novosapolyarny two years ago. She says she has met many interesting people here, and she takes the rigorous regime in the settlement lightly.

'The days are strictly regulated here. We mustn't go for walks at night and we are not allowed to leave the house after 10 pm. Then again, what does that mean, "we are not allowed" – it's recommended not to leave the house. That might be sensible in this extreme climate, and perhaps these rules are good. But what can I do when my heart is singing!'

For Lyosha, a career at Gazprom was the obvious choice. Like many of his colleagues, he comes from what's practically a dynasty of gas workers. His parents and his sister already worked on the Zapolyarnoye field. At the age of 21, Lyosha joined Gazprom, too. He has now been employed by the company as a metalworker for seven years. Before that he was in the air force.

'I served for three years. The financial aspect was the crucial factor in my choice to come here, as is probably the case with most people. The working conditions are good and the job is interesting. What could be improved? The trade unions should have greater influence. And the salary could be even better! That's surely the most burning issue everywhere.'

After initial anti-union campaigns the company-affiliated union Gazprom Profsoyuz was founded 15 years ago. Lyosha is a member, like more than 80 percent of Gazprom employees. An amazing number, signifying wide acceptance among the employees of their workers' representation. However, the Gazprom union is not known for having established itself as a modern and effective organisation that had stood up for the interests of the workforce. Like other company-affiliated unions, it opposes radical actions, instead striving for friendly relations with the company, which in turn supports the union morally and financially.

For most employees the biggest problem with living and working in the North is not the permanent cold and darkness or the strict regulations dictating everyday life, but the long-term separation from family and friends. Even though Skype, Facebook and Twitter bring loved ones a little closer, the yearning for them never stops.

'The hardest part is that my beloved wife is not at my side! It was here that I met her, a shift-change romance, a great love.'

Like Lyosha, Artemi misses his family, too. He too can hardly wait to see them again. A proud new father, he fervently longs for the end of the shift-work period. So far, he has only been able to wave at his new-born son through a webcam. In a few days' time, he will finally be able to hold the 'fine chap', as he already calls him, in his arms.

'Shortly before you go home you get slightly euphoric! That comes from being excited that you have got through the shift and done a good job. And, of course, from wanting to see your loved ones. That desire becomes immeasurable.'

After several weeks of strenuous work the gas workers finally return home, mostly *na zemlju*, to the Big Earth. They recuperate with their families in a milder climate for four to six weeks. Then it's time for another farewell as they return to their shifts in the polar circle.

Eduard Kondratyev and his wife Lena's relationship has been subjected to the rhythm of the monthly shifts for a long time, too. He has commuted from Novy Urengoy to the shift workers camp Novozapolyarny for twelve years. Much as he says he loves his work in the snow desert, the recurrent separation from his family is still hard for him.

'Well, it's just tough not to be by the side of your loved ones. It's awful that I can't witness my child growing up, can't raise her, can't help with her homework. That's bitter, and really hurts.'

While Eduard works on the gas fields, Lena lives in Novy Urengoy with their youngest daughter Katya – not far, really, from her husband's workplace, but out of reach nonetheless. In all these years, Lena hasn't once visited her husband at his work.

The Kondratyev family owns a flat in a prefabricated high-rise, just like almost everyone else in what is one of the richest cities in Russia. Until the transformation of the economic system, the flats were let at moderate rents, but later on, they were put up for sale – they weren't bargains, however. One square metre of living space is worth about 1,500 Euros in the polar circle. The apartment buildings in the city are a stark contrast to the state-of-the-art technology of the gas processing plants. The prefabricated concrete slabs are worn; the piercing cold has clearly left its marks. The buildings lack appropriate thermal insulation. The staircases are dark, damp, and decrepit. Many of the letterboxes in the entrance area are battered and some have been forced open, and the walls are daubed with graffiti. A no-man's-land that nobody feels responsible for.

Behind a heavy iron door lies the cosy flat of the Kondratyevs – their own little paradise. They have turned the standardised two-bedroom apartment into a modern and colourful home. It's very well equipped with a flatscreen TV, a hi-fi system, a little desk area with a computer, a ceramic hob, a dishwasher, and a whirlpool bathtub. The difference between the inside and the outside temperature often amounts to an unbelievable 70 degrees. The centrally controlled gas heating keeps the flat at a comfortable 25 degrees – and that at a fixed price. When it gets too warm, they open a window. An economic use of resources or energy is not a top priority in the gas capital.

'We have got used to Novy Urengoy. When we go on holiday we are drawn back home after a while. The city is my home, although I wasn't born here. My father moved to the North for work. As soon as he had settled in, he brought his family. When I arrived in Novy Urengoy I was amazed how many young people lived here, how many children. There was something special about the people – they were so open-minded and warm.'

Lena Kondratyeva remembers well how her family moved from Chișinău, in today's Moldova, to Novy Urengoy when she was a young girl. The special character of the people, the sweet-naturedness of the *severny chelovek*, the 'Northerner', is mentioned often here in the polar circle.

'People certainly have a more relaxed lifestyle on the Big Earth: there's sunshine, wine, flowers, and the sea. People are different there. Our upbringing is special, it is one of the North. Up here, people move closer together. Their relationships are warmer, friendlier.'

The 'Northerner' is open-minded, companionable and always extremely helpful, Eduard continues. One can only speculate about the reasons. It's probably because it is so difficult to be alone in the Far North.

When Katya braves the bitter cold to leave the house, she likes to go to the Gudzon. The two-storied glass palace is one of several shopping centres in Novy Urengoy. Huge electronics stores and toyshops are lined up next to the branches of well-known fashion chains and the shops for cosmetics and perfumes that can be found in any Western European city. The supermarket is extremely well stocked, offering everything from fresh pasta to Kinder Surprise eggs, from kefir to French cognac, and from papayas and kiwis to organic produce.

While the residents do make use of the various shopping facilities, you wouldn't say that it's particularly busy here. Many tables in the cafes and restaurants remain vacant. There are few window-shoppers, no buskers and, of course, no homeless people or drunks. Neither are there many young people, who you'd expect to come here just to while away the time. Quite astonishing, considering that for nine months of the year, the low temperatures prohibit any kind of public life outdoors, like strolling along the boulevards, or going to the park or the riverbanks. The playgrounds, too, are covered deep in snow. It would seem that the shopping centre would be an ideal place to adopt as a communal space.

Those who are keen on sports or love dancing and singing or the theatre can spend their time in the sports and cultural complex 'Gas Workers', managed by the cultural department of Gazprom Dobycha Urengoy. There is a wide variety of activities and events on offer. The volleyball club 'Flare', which is sponsored by Gazprom, plays its home games here. When there are big celebrations, concerts, or shows, huge crowds flock to the entertainment venue. But who gets to appear on stage and entertain the people is strictly controlled by Gazprom. A member of the theatre group regretfully says that the entertainment programme is subject to stringent supervision. Every project and every guest appearance, she says, has to be approved by the cultural department.

In the shopping centre, in the big sports and cultural complex, and in all the other leisure facilities, everything appears to be strictly organised and controlled. Perhaps people's homes are the only places where they can make their own rules – where the big gas company holds no sway? In any case, when asked what their favourite place in the city is, many residents of Novy Urengoy name their own home.

'My favourite place in Novy Urengoy? My home, of course! When I was a child the most beautiful place on earth was our home. These days I have a cosy nest of my own!'

But no matter whether one's free time is enjoyed with family or friends in the city or simply at home, daily life is determined by work and there is little room for leisure. This is also true for the younger residents, for industriousness and ambition are expected of them, too.

As is the case with so many aspects of life here, the gas industry has a substantial influence on education. Gazprom in particular invests much to ensure a steady supply of qualified young professionals. The technical college, built and financed by Gazprom, is located in the northern district of the city. About 1,000 students study gas extracting technology, plus business administration and accounting, in a four-year course. Internships at the big company are an integral part of the curriculum. In addition to extensive specialist knowledge, great importance is placed on teamwork, flexibility, the ability to deal with stressful situations, a sense of responsibility, and honesty, explains the company spokesman Sergey Chernetsky.

'We are not a charity, we only accept the best of the best. But it is not that we can just live off the fat of the land. We invest a lot into recruiting and retaining new employees. Just recently, many… no, not many, but some skilled employees have moved to independent companies, presumably because they earn more there.'

At the biggest technical universities of the country, in Ufa, Kazan, Krasnodar, Tyumen, Moscow, and St. Petersburg, Gazprom regularly organises events and invites students to the gas capital for an interview to try to sell the idea of a secure and well-paid job in the industry.

But the process of recruiting suitable personnel begins at an even earlier stage: in school. Early on, Gazprom tries to support particularly gifted pupils in an effort to enlist them as potential future employees.

Sixteen-year-old Dima is a fan of German rock music and student in the Gazprom class of the state school in Novy Urengoy. The class was only set up last year; the classroom is painted in the company colours and equipped with the latest technology. Gazprom's gas flare logo is emblazoned above the interactive blackboard. This is where the best of the best are prepared for a potential job at the company.

When the temperature drops below minus 40 degrees, the students are given the day off. They can access the day's tasks and exercises online and send their answers back to the school with a mouse click. Like pupils everywhere, Dima and his classmates are pleased when the lessons are cancelled. On those days, and they aren't all that rare in the polar circle, they can have a lie-in. In short, they are ordinary pupils, except that even at the age of 16 they know quite clearly what they want to be when they grow up, and why.

'If you're in the Gazprom class, you learn more, simply because experts give special lectures that others don't get. Moreover, it's a great opportunity to be able to work for Gazprom. That's a fantastic perspective! The salaries are safe and high. It's the way to a great future.'

A single Gazprom class costs more than 50,000 Euros per year, and there are plans to set up these classes throughout Russia in the near future in order to secure much-needed new recruits. But Gazprom's good reputation as an employer extends beyond technical specialists in the gas industry. Every resident of Novy Urengoy speaks highly of the company.

'You can take pride in being able to say you work for Gazprom.'

Tatyana Borisovna speaks on behalf of her kindergarten team. Gazprom operates eight of the numerous kindergartens in Novy Urengoy. Two of them are part of the special 'prophylaxis' scheme: Belosnezhka – 'Snow White' – in the southern part of Novy Urengoy and Morozko – 'Jack Frost' – in the north. No child has to walk more than a few minutes to its kindergarten. The municipality does much to protect the children in this hostile climate and to compensate for the lack of outdoor activities. Every kindergarten has a gymnasium and a swimming pool, and miniature versions of fields and forests are set up in winter gardens. But Gazprom does even more.

At Morozko, which has previously been recognised as best kindergarten in Russia, a total of 72 nursery teachers, cooks and kitchen helps, paediatricians and ENT specialists, speech therapists and physios look after the well-being of 220 children.

'Preventative medical care for our children is essential. The harsh climate in the North causes damage to the health of children and adults. After all, these conditions are extreme.'

An eye specialist tests the children's eyesight and prescribes the right pair of glasses, if necessary. Speech therapists correct their pronunciation. There are masseurs for one-and-a-half-year-old infants. After a relaxing trip to the sauna, the little ones are served cups of tea at tiny tables, beautifully set. Afterwards they are taken to the playrooms, which are positively crammed with toys. And the cherry on the cake, the thing that makes this kindergarten the best of them all, is the salt chamber: in a cool and darkened room where the walls and ceiling look like those of a grotto, the children lie in their little beds, wearing woolly hats and gloves, watching cartoons and breathing in air that is saturated with salt and other additives for preventing pneumonia. After this, they get a frothy drink.

'We are always battling oxygen deficiency up here in the North. That is why the children get an oxygen cocktail, to supplement what they lack.'

Welcome to 'Starship Morozko'! Of course, whether these oxygen drinks are really necessary is a matter to be disputed – or you could consult the experts. Russian as well as German scientists confirm that the oxygen concentration in the Arctic Circle is not lower than anywhere else in the world. But the oxygen deficiency myth remains part of the life in the North.

'Our army is so strong, so strong, our army is so bold, so bold, our army is so brave, so brave!' – a bright, clear child's voice rings out from the loudspeakers. The anthem echoing through Morozko's hallways is played in honour of the forthcoming Defender of the Fatherland Day, a national holiday. With a jolt, the visitor is transported back from the land of alleged oxygen deficits to what is, after all, a normal Russian kindergarten, where the youngest must already learn to respect the army and love their country.

Much is being invested in the development of Novy Urengoy and the future of its residents. But as far-reaching the projects might be, as extensive the efforts, the viability of the city remains inextricably tied to the natural gas industry. However, nobody in the gas capital is concerned about that. Exhausted deposits or dwindling sources are not an issue. Novy Urengoy will remain Gazprom's important outpost.

'The gas resources certainly decrease from year to year. Some deposits are at their peak now, so that will go on for another five to six years, perhaps. Then the gas production there will decline, but new gas fields will be developed further in the North. However, no new cities will be built, only small settlements for the shift workers. Novy Urengoy will remain the bridgehead.'

Another group affected by the exploitation of new natural gas deposits are the Nenets. They are nomadic reindeer herders, hunters, and fishermen, who live in the Yamalo-Nenets Autonomous Okrug – the area is named after them. Every production plant constitutes a serious interference with nature; the extraction of natural resources leads to environmental damage that endangers the indigenous people, too.

Sergey Chernetsky, the company spokesman, is well aware of this. He talks at length about the good relationship between the gas giant and the Nenets, emphasising how Gazprom tries to compensate for the fact that the grounds the indigenous peoples used as pastures are now built-up. He mentions the settlements for the nomads in the northern part of the region, a boarding school that is sponsored by the company and free education, apprenticeships and training for young Nenets. He adds that they like to celebrate traditional Nenets festivals together, such as the feasts of the reindeer herders and the fishermen. This sounds almost idyllic – but it isn't. Behind the ostensible goodwill lie substantial economic interests. In order to keep up the profitable gas business the industry will follow the gas to ever more remote areas – all the way to the seabed of the Arctic Ocean and its presumed huge gas deposits.

Increasing numbers of people will commute to the North month after month so that the ongoing demand for natural resources is met. But it's not just the new production sites that will provide jobs. Novy Urengoy, too, lures people to the North with the promise of well-paid employment. Doctors and teachers, construction workers and waiters… the gas capital needs everyone. And the municipal building authority must not only maintain the living standard of the inhabitants, it's expected to constantly improve it. Buildings are modernised and extended, and step by step the Subarctic landscape is transformed into urbanised areas.

'We have the difficult task of providing new living space for those who live in very old and damaged houses. This is a highly important task that needs to be completed quickly. The old buildings were put up at great speed, but there was no energy left for considering aesthetics. These days, we try to give the urban districts a special signature to make them less monotonous and dreary. We're also looking into landscaping and greenery; we're building boulevards and parks. All for improving the quality of life in the city.'

In the southern part of the city, where until recently you'd find single-storied timber houses and sheds from the city's early years, the new residential quarter 'Tundra' is arising. It is not substantially different from those built in the socialist era. Five- and nine-storey buildings, rotated and mirrored, are arranged around a spacious courtyard. In the courtyard, within easy walking distance, are a kindergarten and a school. 1,400 families can soon move in. The property developer advertises the advanced construction techniques used, the efficient thermal insulation of the buildings, and the ample available parking. Where in the past developers would have used precast concrete frontages, there are now beige and brown panels, embellished with red canopies, turrets, and decorative gables.

A novelty in the city's urban planning are neighbourhoods with single-family homes. The trend towards a home with a private garden has reached the Arctic Circle, even though that garden can only be used for a few days of the year.

'The situation has changed a bit in recent years. There is a desire for single-family detached houses. This is because people stay longer in the city than initially estimated.'

The urban planner responsible is entrusted with a new task: The development plan provides for quarters with single-family homes in both the southern and the northern parts of the city. It's hard to imagine that bungalows and villas will soon be scattered about the Arctic Circle, each a little fortress in the desert of snow, supplied with heating, electricity and water. But without any doubt, in Gazprom City this, too, is possible.

Today, people might live in Novy Urengoy for decades rather than just a couple of years, but they still don't stay in the Far North forever. They want to return *na zemlju*, to the Big Earth, at the latest by the time they reach retirement. The city in the polar circle is not suitable for life as a pensioner, anyway. After 20 long years of employment, women can go into their well-deserved retirement at the age of 50. Men have to work five years longer. Particularly arduous working conditions might bring forward their retirement by a few years.

'You have worked diligently and at a high level. So you can leave with your head held high. You have undoubtedly earned all you ever wanted. You get it all. You gain recognition and you are decorated with medals, certificates, and awards. In short: if you work hard, you can thoroughly enjoy your retirement years.'

Thus dream most people of leaving the city at old age. They dream of a life hereafter. And Gazprom has included this dream in the life script for its employees. The company offers a long-term savings scheme for financing housing 'in Russia'. The employees only have to contribute a small part. They can fully focus on their aspirations for their dream house. It's a much-discussed topic at many kitchen tables in Novy Urengoy during the long winter months, with the deliberations including the drawing up of concrete plans. The dreams of the employees of the world's biggest gas extracting enterprise are not out of this world: they are firmly down to native earth.

'Do I already have plans for my retirement? Well, the most important thing is to build a house, a villa. It should definitely have two floors, so that my children and grandchildren can come visit me anytime, and everybody can have their own little corner. I will have a big dog in my house and a watchdog outside. Yes, we will have two dogs, and a cat, too, and a huge fish tank. I will design a garden with flowers, berries, and bushes – but no potato patch! A place where you can put a table and some chairs down, and a samovar, and you drink tea in the evening and the children are running around, and when it's hot, you can take a dip in the pool. And somewhere there's a barbecue, too, and the whole family gets together there. It should be so cosy that everybody always loves to come home.'

Mikrorajon Mirny
Микрорайон Мирный
Microrayon Mirny

Zwischen Nowy Urengoi und UKPG-16 II
Между Новым Уренгоем и УКПГ-16 II
Between Novy Urengoy and UKPG-16 II

1. Mikrorajon
1-й микрорайон
1st Microrayon

Pontonbrücke über den Fluss Pur
Понтонный мост через реку Пур
Pontoon bridge across the River Pur

Internationalnaja-Straße 1e
Улица Интернациональная 1e
Internationalnaya Street 1e

Treppenhaus im Plattenbau
Подъезд в жилом здании
Housing block staircase

Aufbereitungsanlage UKPG-2S, Sapoljarnoje I
УКПГ-2С, Заполярное I
Gas treatment unit UKPG-2S, Zapolyarnoye I

Leningradski Prospekt
Ленинградский проспект
Leningradsky Prospekt

Fleischmarkt I
Мясной рынок I
Meat market I

Zwischen Nowy Urengoi und Sapoljarnoje I
Между Новым Уренгоем и Заполярным I
Between Novy Urengoy and Zapolyarnoye I

Zwischen Nowy Urengoi und Sapoljarnoje II
Между Новым Уренгоем и Заполярным II
Between Novy Urengoy and Zapolyarnoye II

Schichtarbeitersiedlung Nowosapoljarny
Вахтовый посёлок Новозаполярный
Novozapolyarny shift workers camp

Mikrorajon Sowjetski
Микрорайон Советский
Microrayon Sovetsky

Zwischen Nowy Urengoi und Sapoljarnoje III
Между Новым Уренгоем и Заполярным III
Between Novy Urengoy and Zapolyarnoye III

Wintergarten, Nowosapoljarny
Зимний сад, Новозаполярный
Winter garden, Novozapolyarny

Aufenthaltsraum, Wohnkomplex in Nowosapoljarny
Комната отдыха, жилой модуль Новозаполярный
Lounge, apartment complex in Novozapolyarny

Aufenthaltsraum, Wohnkomplex bei UKPG-16
Комната отдыха, жилой модуль УКПГ-16
Lounge, apartment complex near UKPG-16

Spielplatz, Kindergarten Morosko
Детская площадка, детский сад Морозко
Playground, Morozko kindergarten

Förderbohrungen Abschnitt Nr. 207, Sapoljarnoje
Куст газовых скважин № 207, Заполярное
Gas wells section No. 207, Zapolyarnoye

Straße der Freundschaft der Völker
Улица Дружбы народов
Street of the Friendship of the Peoples

Aufbereitungsanlage UKPG-2S, Sapoljarnoje II
УКПГ-2С, Заполярное II
Gas treatment unit UKPG-2S, Zapolyarnoye II

Kontrollraum, UKPG-16
Диспетчерская, УКПГ-16
Control room, UKPG-16

Am Stadtrand
На окраине города
Edge of town

Hauptplatz
Городская площадь
Main square

Kultur- und Sportkomplex, Nowosapoljarny
Культурно-спортивный комплекс, Новозаполярный
Sports and cultural centre, Novozapolyarny

Fleischmarkt II
Мясной рынок II
Meat market II

Erinnerungen eines Pioniers
INTERVIEW MIT WLADIMIR TAMPLON

Der 69-jährige Wladimir Tamplon, geboren 1946 in Buguruslan, in der westlichen Oblast Orenburg, auf halber Strecke zwischen den Städten Samara und Ufa, war einer der ersten Siedler in Nowy Urengoi.

Heute leben er und seine Familie in Dortmund. In wenigen Wochen kehrt er als Gast zurück in den Norden, zur Feier des 40. Jubiläums der Stadt. Er erinnert sich an seine Zeit am Polarkreis, und er erzählt begeistert davon, so als wäre es gestern gewesen.

In welchem Jahr sind Sie nach Nowy Urengoi übersiedelt?
Das war im März 1977, ich war damals 31 Jahre alt.

Wie haben Sie von der Möglichkeit gehört, an den Polarkreis zu ziehen, und was war schlussendlich der Grund, sich tatsächlich für den Umzug zu entscheiden?
Das hat sich ganz einfach durch meinen Beruf ergeben. Wer in der Erdgas- oder Erdölindustrie arbeitet, weiß, wo neue Felder gefunden werden. Ich habe davon gehört, und es klang interessant. Gelockt hat mich hauptsächlich das Interesse an einer neuen Aufgabe, die Arbeit auf einem neuen Bohrfeld, gemeinsam mit neuen Leuten. Wir waren damals ganz wenige, nur zwei Bohrbrigaden. Wir haben uns als Pioniere gesehen.

Hat auch das Einkommen eine Rolle gespielt?
Ja, wir haben wahrscheinlich den fünffachen Monatslohn bekommen. Dort waren ja auch ganz andere Bedingungen – die Kälte, die Entfernung. [1]

Was war Ihre erste Aufgabe?
Als ich in Nowy Urengoi angekommen bin, habe ich bei Gazprom als Bohrmeister gearbeitet, also damals war es ja noch ein Ministerium. Später wurde daraus Gazprom, und ich habe dort andere Posten bekommen, in leitenden Positionen. Es gab mit der Zeit immer mehr Möglichkeiten und auch andere Firmen. Trotzdem gab es aber immer genügend Arbeit für alle und keine Konkurrenz. Ich hatte nie Schwierigkeiten.

Sind Sie alleine nach Nowy Urengoi gezogen?
Ich war damals schon verheiratet und hatte auch zwei Kinder – doch zunächst bin ich alleine nach Nowy Urengoi gezogen. Meine Familie ist erst später gekommen, meine Frau und die Töchter, damals fünf und acht Jahre alt.

Was hat ihre Familie, was haben ihre Freunde zu dem Entschluss gesagt, an den Polarkreis zu ziehen?
Was konnten sie schon sagen? Das Ziel war, neue Arbeit zu finden. Meiner Familie ist nichts anderes übrig geblieben. Sie waren natürlich sehr aufgeregt. Doch es ist alles gut gegangen. Als ich dann in Nowy Urengoi war, habe ich meine Schwester und meinen Bruder eingeladen – sie sind dann auch gekommen und haben dort Arbeit gefunden. Meine Schwester war im Heizwerk beschäftigt. Sie hatte nichts mit der Erdgasförderung zu tun.

Wurde Ihr Umzug an den Polarkreis vom Staat organisiert?
Nein. Es gab keine Unterstützung, obwohl es schwer war dorthin zu kommen – also Nowy Urengoi war damals einfach schwer zu erreichen. Es gab noch keine Straßen und der erste Zug ist erst im August 1982 in der Stadt angekommen. Die Anreise war für lange Zeit nur mit dem Flugzeug möglich, ein Ticket von Moskau nach Nowy Urengoi hat früher aber fast nichts gekostet.

Wie sah Nowy Urengoi damals aus? Welche Situation haben Sie am Polarkreis vorgefunden?
Es gab noch keine Stadt! Es waren nur Fachleute dort, und man konnte nur mit einer Einladung dorthin kommen. Die Situation war schlecht, also es war schwer. Aber wir waren noch jung, alles war interessant. Zu Beginn haben vielleicht 500 bis 600 Leute dort gewohnt, also nur ganz wenige. Die Infrastruktur musste erst aufgebaut werden, es gab noch keine richtigen Wohnungen. Was es gab, waren die sogenannten „Fässer". [2] Doch jeden Tag wurde etwas gebaut, die ersten Siedlungen aus Holzbaracken entstanden, weit weg von dort, wo die Wohnviertel heute sind. Beim 30-jährigen Jubiläum der Stadt standen sogar noch viele dieser selbstgebauten Hütten, jetzt sind schon fast alle weg.

Wo haben Sie nach Ihrer Ankunft gewohnt?
Eigentlich ging alles ganz schnell. Ich bin nach Nowy Urengoi gezogen und dann sind auch schon die anderen gekommen, alle gemeinsam haben wir in einem „Fass" gelebt – meine Familie und die Familie meiner Schwester, ihr Mann und mein Neffe Eduard. Im „Fass" haben wir ungefähr zwei Jahre lang gewohnt, dann wurden die ersten zweistöckigen Häuser gebaut, aus

Holz, und ich habe meine erste Wohnung bekommen. Ab 1980 kamen Bauunternehmen und haben mehrstöckige Häuser gebaut, ich bin wieder umgezogen: in ein fünfstöckiges Haus, in eine Wohnung mit vier Zimmern.

War das Leben am Polarkreis eine Herausforderung?
Wissen Sie, zwölf Jahre lang habe ich kein freies Wochenende gehabt, es gab immer nur Arbeit und noch mehr Arbeit. Wir haben nur Interesse an der Arbeit gehabt. Das war alles damals. Heute geht es den Menschen dort sehr gut. Erst gab es nichts, und als ich weggezogen bin, war da eine riesige Stadt. Alles ist so schnell gewachsen. Mittlerweile hat man viel gemacht für die Bewohner, es gibt Geschäfte, Parks und vieles mehr. Die Menschen verdienen gut, die jungen Leute, die in Nowy Urengoi aufwachsen, bekommen eine gute Ausbildung.

Haben Sie jemals bereut, in den hohen Norden gezogen zu sein?
Nein, auf keinen Fall. Ich habe dort ein gutes Leben gehabt, obwohl ich Tag und Nacht gearbeitet habe. Meine Frau war Lehrerin, sie hat nach dem Umzug nach Nowy Urengoi an der ersten Schule der Stadt gearbeitet, dort war sie später dann sogar Direktorin.

Wann und warum sind Sie aus Nowy Urengoi weggezogen?
Das war 1992. Es ist so – ich habe einen deutschen Pass, also ich hatte auch damals schon, wegen meiner Herkunft, so etwas wie einen deutschen Pass. [3] Nach Auflösung der Sowjetunion, als Jelzin an die Macht kam, wurden die Gebietsansprüche der ehemals deutschen Siedler neu diskutiert. Daraufhin kam es zu Protestaktionen der russischen Bevölkerung. Ich habe davon gelesen und zu meiner Frau gesagt: „Jetzt reicht's! Wir ziehen nach Deutschland. Es kann eine Zeit kommen, die für uns Schwierigkeiten bringt. Wir sollten wegziehen". Das war noch vor dem Rentenalter, ich war 46 Jahre alt. Wir sind also nach Deutschland gezogen, und ich habe hier gearbeitet bis zum Ruhestand. Die Rente habe ich dann hier beantragt, obwohl ich es auch in Russland hätte machen können. Von Gazprom bekomme ich heute nichts.

Haben Sie noch Verbindungen zur Stadt, zu Leuten, die heute dort leben?
Mit vielen Menschen, die ich dort kennengelernt habe, bin ich immer noch befreundet. Sie sind alle schon weggezogen, an unterschiedliche Orte. Wir alle sehen uns aber auch heute noch oft, in St. Petersburg, Rostow oder in Moskau. Nur Eduard, mein Neffe, ist immer noch dort – aber er ist noch jung. Alle meine Freunde sind in Rente, keiner von ihnen lebt noch in Nowy Urengoi. Man darf schon in der Stadt bleiben, aber was soll man dort machen?

Vermissen Sie Nowy Urengoi?
Ja. Ich vermisse die Stadt, ich vermisse meine Arbeit.

Was passiert mit der Stadt, wenn die Gasvorkommen zur Neige gehen?
Es wird eine Stadt sein, von der aus man weiterfliegt und andere Erdgasfelder bearbeitet. Im Norden gibt es noch so viele Möglichkeiten! Wir haben damals bis zu einer Tiefe von 1.300 Metern gebohrt, heute bohrt man bis 3.000 Meter. Es gibt noch viele Reserven – die Stadt hat noch sehr viel vor!

Ist Europa Ihrer Meinung nach von Erdgasimporten aus Russland abhängig?
Es ist eine Abhängigkeit auf Wunsch der einzelnen Regierungen. Es gibt ja heute mehrere Möglichkeiten, Erdgas zu importieren, aber diese Abhängigkeit wurde noch zu Sowjetzeiten besiegelt. Es wurden Langzeitverträge geschlossen und man hat Leitungen nach Europa gelegt, die durch diese Abkommen finanziert wurden. Ich erinnere mich an den 22. April 1978, an die Verträge, die damals mit Deutschland geschlossen wurden, über den Bau neuer Trassen und Erdgaslieferungen für mehr als 25 Jahre. Das war ein Anreiz! Zu dieser Zeit hat das Erdgas der Sowjetunion Devisen und Investitionen westlicher Konzerne eingebracht. Das Gas dafür kam von meinen Bohrlöchern! [4]

Was bedeutet Gazprom für Sie?
Meine Heimat! Mein ganzes Leben habe ich bei Gazprom gearbeitet.

Welche Eindrücke vom Leben im Norden sind Ihnen in besonderer Erinnerung geblieben?
Ich glaube, man behält nur das Beste von dem, was war, das Schlimme vergisst man. Alles war besonders! Ich erinnere mich einfach an die schöne Zeit, als ich dort gearbeitet und gelebt habe. Unsere Familie hat Gutes geleistet. In diesem Jahr wurden wir eingeladen, um zum 40. Jubiläum nach Nowy Urengoi zu kommen. Die Stadtverwaltung hat uns noch nicht vergessen!

Воспоминания первопроходца
ИНТЕРВЬЮ С ВЛАДИМИРОМ ТАМПЛОНОМ

Владимиру Тамплону 69 лет, он родился в 1946 году в Бугуруслане, на западе Оренбургской области, на полпути между Самарой и Уфой. Владимир был одним из первых поселенцев Нового Уренгоя.

Теперь он со своей семьёй живёт в Дортмунде. Через несколько недель Владимир вернётся в Новый Уренгой на празднование 40-летнего юбилея города. Он вспоминает тогдашнюю жизнь близ Полярного Круга с восхищением, как будто это было еще вчера.

В каком году вы переселились в Новый Уренгой?
В марте 1977 года, мне был тогда 31 год.

Как вы узнали о возможности переселения в Приполярье и что в конце концов повлияло на ваше решение?
Всё произошло благодаря моей профессии. Те, кто работают в газовой или нефтедобывающей отрасли, узнают об открытии новых месторождений. Я услышал об этом, и мне захотелось туда съездить. Меня привлёк по большей части интерес к новым задачам, разработка нового месторождения вместе с новыми людьми. Нас было тогда совсем мало, только две бригады бурильщиков. Мы считали себя первопроходцами.

Заработок также играл для вас важную роль?
Да, мы зарабатывали примерно в пять раз больше обычного. Там всё-таки были совсем другие условия: холод и удалённость. [1]

Кем вы работали в первое время?
По приезду в Новый Уренгой, я работал в Газпроме буровым мастером. Тогда это было ещё министерство. Потом оно преобразовалось в Газпром и я занимал там различные руководящие посты. Со временем появлялось много разнообразных возможностей и разных фирм. Тем не менее, работы было всегда достаточно для всех, тогда не было никакой конкуренции. У меня не было никаких трудностей.

Вы переехали в Новый Уренгой один?
Я был тогда женат и у меня было уже двое детей, однако сначала я переехал один. Моя семья приехала позже: жена с двумя дочерьми, тогда им было пять и восемь лет.

Как ваша семья и друзья отнеслись к решению переехать жить в Приполярье?
Что они могли сказать? Главное было найти новую работу. Моей семье не оставалось другого выбора, как последовать за мной. Они конечно очень переживали, но дела у нас скоро пошли на лад. Потом я пригласил в Новый Уренгой своих сестру и брата, они тоже приехали и нашли себе там работу. Сестра работала на теплоцентрали, не в газовой отрасли.

Помогло ли вам государство с переездом в Приполярье?
Нет, никакой поддержки не было, хотя туда было очень трудно добраться. Тогда не было ещё никаких дорог, а первый поезд прибыл в город только в августе 1982 года. Долгое время туда можно было добраться только самолётом. Правда, билет от Москвы до Нового Уренгоя тогда почти ничего не стоил.

Как выглядел тогда Новый Уренгой? Каким предстало перед вами Приполярье?
Тогда ещё не было никакого города. Там были только специалисты, в город можно было приехать только по приглашению. Ситуация была трудной, но мы были молодыми и нам всё было интересно. Сначала нас было всего 500–600 человек, совсем немного. Перво-наперво надо было наладить инфраструктуру: у нас не было нормальных квартир, мы жили в «бочках». [2] Однако каждый день что-нибудь строилось, первые посёлки из деревянных бараков возникли далеко от того места, где сейчас расположены жилые кварталы. Ещё на тридцатилетний юбилей города можно было увидеть много таких деревянных хибар, сегодня же их почти не осталось.

Где вы жили после приезда?
Собственно говоря, мы обустроились довольно быстро. Я приехал в Новый Уренгой, а там уже и другие прибыли, все вместе мы жили в «бочке»: моя семья, сестра со своим мужем и моим племянником Эдуардом. В «бочке» мы прожили примерно два года, к тому времени были построены первые двухэтажные деревянные дома, в одном из них я и получил свою первую квартиру. В 1980 году в городе появились первые строительные предприятия и началось строительство многоэтажек. Я опять переехал, на этот раз в пятиэтажку, в четырёхкомнатную квартиру.

Жизнь близ Полярного Круга стала для вас тяжёлым испытанием?

Знаете, на протяжении двенадцати лет у меня не было выходных. Была только работа и ещё раз работа. Нас интересовала только работа, она была для нас всем. Сегодня людям там очень хорошо живётся. Когда я туда приехал, то увидел пустошь, а когда уезжал, на этом месте стоял уже огромный город. Он вырос очень быстро, очень многое было сделано для его жителей — были построены магазины, обустроены парки и многое другое. Люди хорошо зарабатывают, молодёжь Нового Уренгоя получает хорошее образование.

Вам когда-нибудь приходилось жалеть о своем переезде на Крайний север?

Нет, никогда. У меня там была хорошая жизнь, хотя я работал день и ночь. Моя жена была учительницей в первой Новоуренгойской школе. Позже она дослужилась до директора.

Когда и почему вы уехали из Нового Уренгоя?

В 1992 году. У меня есть немецкий паспорт, в общем, у меня тогда уже, благодаря моим корням, было что-то вроде немецкого паспорта. [3] После распада Советского Союза, когда пришёл к власти Ельцин, среди немецких колонистов возобновились разговоры о том, что пора возвратиться назад в свои дома, на свои земли. В связи с этим начались протесты со стороны русского населения. Я прочитал об этом и сказал жене: «Хватит! Мы уезжаем в Германию. Могут настать такие времена, что нам придётся туго. Надо уезжать». До пенсии было ещё далеко, мне было тогда 46 лет. В общем, мы уехали в Германию, я проработал тут до пенсии. Документы на получение пенсии я подал здесь, хотя мог бы это сделать и в России. От Газпрома я не получаю сегодня ни копейки.

У вас остались связи с городом, с людьми, которые там живут?

Со многими из тех, с кем я там познакомился, я дружу до сих пор. Они уже все разъехались по разным городам. Однако мы часто встречаемся в Петербурге, Ростове или Москве. Только Эдуард, мой племянник, остался там, но он ещё молод. Все мои друзья уже пенсионеры и никого из них в Новом Уренгое не осталось. Конечно, можно было бы остаться, вот только чем там заняться?

Вы скучаете по Новому Уренгою?

Да, я скучаю по городу, мне не хватает моей работы.

Что станет с городом, когда запасы природного газа подойдут к концу?

Город станет отправным пунктом, из которого можно будет добираться до новых месторождений. У Крайнего севера есть большой потенциал! Мы тогда бурили скважины на 1 300 метров, сегодня их бурят на глубину до 3 000 метров. Есть ещё резервы — у города ещё многое впереди!

Как вы думаете, Европа зависима от импорта российского газа?

Эта зависимость создаётся по воле отдельных правительств. Сегодня газ можно импортировать из различных источников, но эта зависимость установилась ещё с советских времён. Ещё тогда были заключены долгосрочные договоры и были проложены трубопроводы в Европу, их прокладка финансировалась благодаря этим соглашениям. Я вспоминаю 22 апреля 1978 года, когда были заключены договоры с Германией на прокладку новых трасс для трубопроводов и на поставку газа, сроком более чем на 25 лет. Это стало настоящим событием! Тогда природный газ приносил Советскому Союзу валюту и инвестиции от западных концернов. И этот был газ из моих скважин! [4]

Что значит для вас Газпром?

Это моя родина. Я проработал в Газпроме всю свою жизнь.

Остались ли у вас какие-то особенные впечатления от жизни на Крайнем севере?

Я думаю, в памяти остаётся только хорошее, плохое забывается. Всё было особенным! Я вспоминаю о золотых временах, когда я там работал и жил. Наша семья многого добилась. В этом году мы снова приглашены в Новый Уренгой, на 40-летний юбилей города. Городское начальство нас ещё не забыло.

Memories of a Pionieer
INTERVIEW WITH VLADIMIR TAMPLON

Vladimir Tamplon, 69 years old, was born in Buguruslan in 1946. The town is situated in the western Orenburg Oblast, halfway between the cities of Samara and Ufa. He was one of the first settlers in Novy Urengoy.

Today, he and his family live in Dortmund. In a few weeks he will return to the North as a guest of the 40th-anniversary celebrations of the city. He still has vivid memories of his time in the Far North and talks passionately about it, as if it were only yesterday.

When did you move to Novy Urengoy?
It was in March 1977 at the age of 31.

How did you learn that it was possible to relocate to the Arctic Circle and what was your ultimate reason for choosing to move there?
That simply arose from my profession. Whoever works in the natural gas or crude oil industry knows where new fields are discovered. I heard about the new field at Novy Urengoy, and it sounded interesting. It was primarily the new assignment that attracted me, working at a new drilling field, and working with new people. We were only a few workers then, only two drilling teams, and we felt like real pioneers.

Did the salary also play a role?
It did indeed. We probably earned five times the average monthly wage. But the conditions were extreme… the cold, you know, the long distance from home. [1]

What was your first task?
When I came to Novy Urengoy I worked with Gazprom as a drillmaster. Well, back then it was still a government department. But later it became Gazprom, and I got different positions there, leading roles. By and by more possibilities opened up, and different companies arrived, too. There was always plenty of work for everybody, though, and no competition. I never had any difficulties.

Did you move to Novy Urengoy on your own?
I was already married by that time and had two children, but at first I moved to Novy Urengoy alone. My beloved family, that is my wife and my two daughters, came later. My daughters were five and eight years old then.

What did your family and your friends say to your decision to move to the Arctic Circle?
What could they say? The objective was to find a new job. My family had no other choice. Of course, they were anxious, but everything went smoothly. When I had settled in Novy Urengoy I invited my brother and my sister to join me. And they did, and both found a job. My sister worked in a heating station; she had nothing to do with the production of natural gas.

Was your relocation to the polar circle organised by the government?
No, not at all. There was no support whatsoever, although it was very difficult to get there. I mean, Novy Urengoy was complicated to reach. There were no roads, and trains didn't run until August 1982. For a long time getting to the city was only possible by plane. But a flight ticket from Moscow to Novy Urengoy cost practically nothing.

What did Novy Urengoy look like at that time? What was the situation in the Arctic when you arrived?
At that time, there was no city at all. Only specialists lived there, and you needed an invitation to get there. The situation was rather bad, I mean, it was all very difficult, but we were young and ambitious and everything was interesting. In the beginning only few people lived there, between 500 and 600. The entire infrastructure had to be built and there was no proper housing. There were only these 'barrels'. [2] But every day we built something new. The first residential areas were built, all wooden shacks, far from where the residential quarters are today. At the 30th anniversary of the city, many of those wooden huts were still standing, but by now nearly all of them have disappeared.

When you arrived in Novy Urengoy, where did you live?
Actually, everything went very quickly. I moved to Novy Urengoy, and the whole family followed after a short time. We all lived in one of those 'barrels' together – my family and my sister's family, her husband and my nephew Eduard. We lived in the 'barrel' for about two years, then the first two-storey wooden houses were built and I got my first real flat. As of 1980, construction companies arrived and they put up multistorey houses. I moved into a five-storey building and had a three-bedroom flat.

Would you say that it was challenging to live in the Arctic Circle?

You know, I didn't have a free weekend for twelve years. There was only work and more work. We weren't interested in anything else, either. That was all there was in those times. Today, the people in Novy Urenoy lead a good life. There was virtually nothing there at the beginning, but when I moved away, there was a huge city. It grew very quickly. Much has been done for the residents. The city has a lot to offer: shops, parks, and many other things. People earn well, the young people who grow up in Novy Urengoy get a good education.

Did you ever regret having moved to the Far North?

No, not at all. I had a good life up there, although I did work day and night. My wife was a teacher, and after moving to Novy Urengoy she worked at the first school of the city. Later she was even appointed headmistress.

When and why did you leave Novy Urengoy?

That was in 1992. I have a German passport... back then I already had sort of a German passport because of my ancestry. [3] When Yeltsin came into power after the dissolution of the Soviet Union, the territorial claims of the former German settlers came to be disputed. As a result, there were protests among the Russian population. When I read about this, I said to my wife, 'That's it! Let's go to Germany. There may come a time that brings us trouble. We better move.' That was before I'd reached retirement age, I was 46 years old then. So we moved to Germany. I have worked here until retirement. I claimed my pension in Germany, although I could have also claimed it in Russia. I don't get anything from Gazprom.

Do you remain connected with the city, are you in contact with people who still live there?

I am still friends with many people I met there, but they have all already moved to different places. But we still meet from time to time, in St. Petersburg, in Rostov or in Moscow. Only Eduard, my nephew, still lives up there – but he is still young. All my friends have already retired and don't live in Novy Urengoy anymore. Of course, you could stay there, but what would you be doing there?

Do you miss Novy Urengoy?

Yes, certainly. I miss the city and I miss my work.

What will happen to Novy Urengoy when the gas resources run out?

It will be a city that is used as a base from which to fly out to develop other gas fields. There are still so many possibilities in the North! We used to drill to a depth of 1,300 metres, but nowadays you drill down to 3,000 metres. There are still many deposits, and there are lots of plans for the city.

In your opinion, does Europe depend on natural gas imports from Russia?

The dependence is a result of the wishes of individual European governments. Today, there are several possibilities to import natural gas, but the dependence on Russian gas imports was sealed during the Soviet era. Long-term contracts were entered into and new gas pipelines were laid, financed by those contracts. I still remember the 22 April 1978, when the contracts with Germany for the supply of natural gas and the construction of new pipeline routes were signed, with a term of more than 25 years. That was a real incentive! It brought foreign exchange to the Soviet Union and capital investment by Western companies. And the gas came from my boreholes! [4]

What does Gazprom mean to you?

It's my home! I have worked for Gazprom all my life.

Which parts of life in the North have left a particularly strong impression on you?

I think you only remember the good things and forget the bad ones. Everything was special! I just remember the good times when I worked and lived there. My family did a good job. This year we have been invited to Novy Urengoy to celebrate the city's 40th anniversary. The municipality hasn't forgotten us yet!

[1]
Die sowjetischen Behörden haben die freiwillige Umsiedlung in den hohen Norden mit finanziellen und materiellen Anreizen wie auch zusätzlichen Sozialleistungen gefördert.

Советское правительство финансово поощряло добровольное переселение на Крайний Север так называемыми «северными надбавками».

The Soviet authorities promoted the voluntary relocation to the North through financial and material incentives, as well as supplementary social benefits.

[2]
Die sogenannten „Fässer" bezeichnen röhrenförmige, waggonähnliche Behausungen aus Metall, die den ersten Siedlern zur Verfügung gestellt wurden. Mehrere dieser Wohneinheiten wurden zu „Fass-Städtchen" angeordnet, den *wagon gorodok*.

Так называемые «бочки» представляли собой бочкообразные жилища из металла, которые предоставляли первым переселенцам в качестве временного жилья. Большое число таких «бочек» считалось поселением, их называли «вагон-городками».

The so-called 'barrels' that were provided for the first settlers were tubular dwellings from metal, similar to railway carriages. A number of these residential units were grouped together to make up small 'barrel towns': the *vagon gorodok*.

[3]
Aufgrund der wolgadeutschen Herkunft von Wladimir Tamplon war in seinem sowjetischen Pass beim Nationalitäteneintrag „Deutsch" angeführt.

В силу немецкого происхождения, в графе «национальность» советского паспорта Владимира Тамплона стояло «немец».

Due to Tamplon's Volga-German ancestry, his nationality was denoted as 'German' in his Soviet passport.

[4]
Hier wird die deutsch-russische Erdgaspartnerschaft angesprochen, aus der Langzeitverträge über Erdgaslieferungen zwischen der Sowjetunion und der DDR bzw. der BRD hervorgegangen sind. Der 22. April 1978 markiert den Beginn der industriellen Gasförderung in der Lagerstätte Urengoi.

Речь идет о советско-германском соглашении по добыче газа, по результатом которого СССР заключило долгосрочные договоры на поставку газа с ГДР и ФРГ. 22 апреля 1978 года считается началом промышленной разработки Уренгойского газового месторождения.

Tamplon refers to the German-Soviet natural gas partnership and the resulting long-term contracts for the supply of natural gas of the Soviet Union with the German Democratic Republic and with the Federal Republic of Germany. The 22 April 1978 marks the beginning of industrial gas production at the Urengoy gas field.

Nowy Urengoi
Новый Уренгой
Novy Urengoy

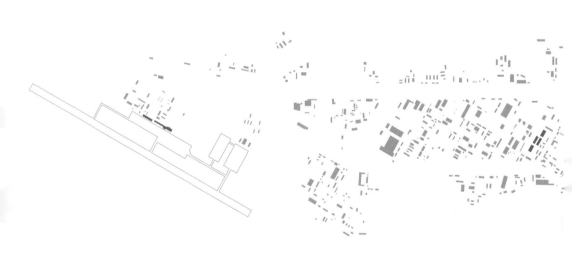

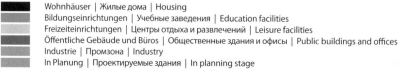

Wohnhäuser | Жилые дома | Housing
Bildungseinrichtungen | Учебные заведения | Education facilities
Freizeiteinrichtungen | Центры отдыха и развлечений | Leisure facilities
Öffentliche Gebäude und Büros | Общественные здания и офисы | Public buildings and offices
Industrie | Промзона | Industry
In Planung | Проектируемые здания | In planning stage

Entdeckung des Urengoi-Gasfeldes
Открытие месторождения Уренгойское
Discovery of the Urengoy gas field

Regelmäßige Flüge von Nowy Urengoi nach Moskau
Регулярные авиарейсы Новый Уренгой-Москва
Regular flights from Novy Urengoy to Moscow

Ankunft der ersten Erdgasarbeiter
Прибытие первых газовиков
Arrival of the first gas workers

Bau der Pipeline „Bruderschaft"
Строительство газопровода «Братство»
Construction of the 'Brotherhood' pipeline

Die Eisenbahntrasse erreicht die Stadt,
die Verbindung zur Großen Erde steht
Железная дорога к городу проложена;
связь с Большой землёй установлена
The railway tracks to the city are completed,
Novy Urengoy is connected to the Big Earth

Erste Erdgaslieferungen erreichen Westeuropa
Первые поставки газа из Уренгоя в Западную Европу
Natural gas from Urengoy reaches Western Europe

Erstellung eines Stadtentwicklungsplans – Erwartung: 200.000 Einwohner bis 2010
Создание плана развития города на 200 000 жителей к 2010 году
A City Development Plan is drawn up – population projection: 200,000 by 2010

Nowy Urengoi erhält den Stadt-Status
Новому Уренгою присвоен статус города
Novy Urengoy is granted city status

| 1966 | - - - | 1973 | | 1975 | | | | 1980 | | | | 1985 | | | | 1990 | | |

Das Gasfeld Jamburg wird erschlossen
Эксплуатация Ямбургского месторождения
Start of the exploitation of the Yamburg gas field

1. Wahlen der „Miss Urengoy"
1. Выборы «Мисс Уренгой»
1. 'Miss Urengoy' beauty contest

Beginn der industriellen Gasförderung auf dem Urengoi-Gasfeld
Начало промышленной газодобычи на Уренгойском месторождении
Start of the industrial exploitation of the Urengoy gas field

Die ersten Kinder werden in der Stadt geboren
В городе родились первые дети
The first children are born in the city

Eröffnung der ersten Schule
Открытие первой школы
The first primary school is opened

Das erste Gymnasium wird eröffnet
Открытие первой городской гимназии
The first secondary school is opened

40-jähriges Jubiläum der Stadt
40-летний юбилей города
40th anniversary of the city

Einwohner: 115.092
Durchschnittsalter: 32
Das Durchschnittseinkommen ist 6,3 mal höher als das festgelegte Existenzminimum in Russland
Жители: 115 092
Средний возраст: 32
Среднемесячная зарплата в 6,3 раза выше прожиточного минимума в России
Inhabitants: 115,092
Average age: 32
The average monthly income is 6.3 times higher than the official living wage in Russia

Erste demokratische Bürgermeisterwahlen
Состоялись первые демократические выборы мэра
First democratic mayoral election

Industriell gefördertes Gas des Sapoljarnoje-Feldes erreicht Nowy Urengoi
Первые поставки газа с месторождения Заполярное в Новый Уренгой
Industrially produced gas from the Zapolyarnoye field reaches Novy Urengoy

| 1995 | | | | 2000 | | | | 2005 | | | | 2010 | | | | **2015** |

Urengoygazprom übergibt die Verantwortung für den Bau von Wohnraum,
kommunalen Einrichtungen und Infrastruktur an die Stadt
Весь жилищный фонд, объекты коммунальной и инженерной инфраструктуры
перешли от ООО «Уренгойгазпром» в муниципальную собственность
Urengoygazprom passes on responsibility for the development of housing,
communal facilities, and infrastructure to the municipality

Seit der Erschließung des Urengoi-Gasfeldes wurden 6,5 Billionen Kubikmeter Erdgas gefördert
Совокупная добыча газа на Уренгойском месторождении составила 6,5 триллионов кубометров
6.5 trillion cubic metres of gas have been produced since the beginning of the development of the Urengoy gas field

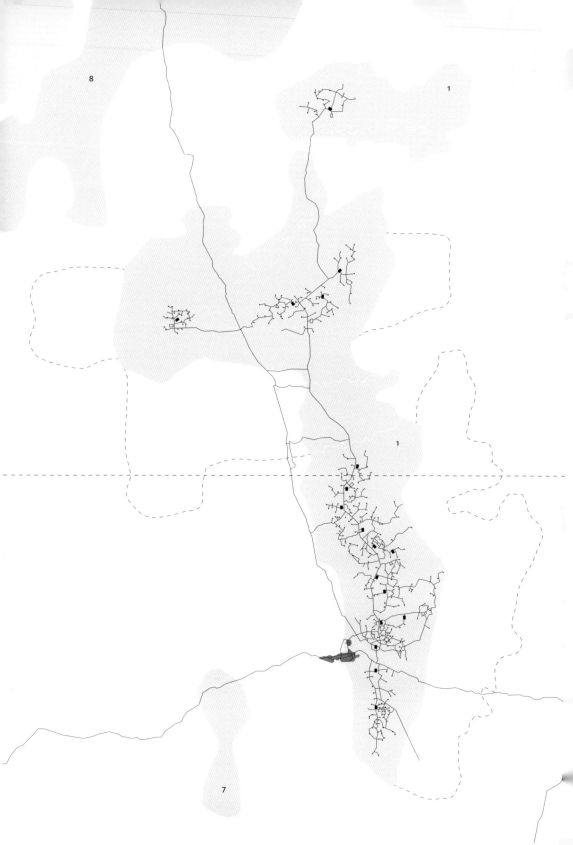

Erdgasfelder
Газовые месторождения
Natural gas fields

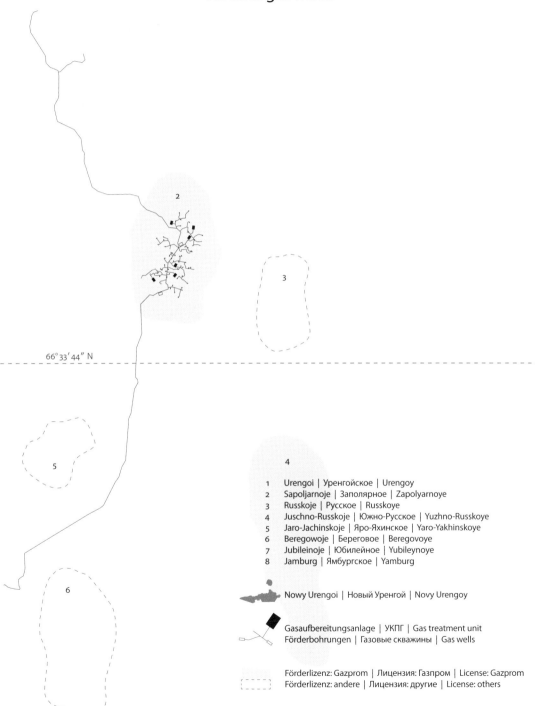

66° 33′ 44″ N

2

3

5

4

6

1   Urengoi | Уренгойское | Urengoy
2   Sapoljarnoje | Заполярное | Zapolyarnoye
3   Russkoje | Русское | Russkoye
4   Juschno-Russkoje | Южно-Русское | Yuzhno-Russkoye
5   Jaro-Jachinskoje | Яро-Яхинское | Yaro-Yakhinskoye
6   Beregowoje | Береговое | Beregovoye
7   Jubileinoje | Юбилейное | Yubileynoye
8   Jamburg | Ямбургское | Yamburg

Nowy Urengoi | Новый Уренгой | Novy Urengoy

Gasaufbereitungsanlage | УКПГ | Gas treatment unit
Förderbohrungen | Газовые скважины | Gas wells

Förderlizenz: Gazprom | Лицензия: Газпром | License: Gazprom
Förderlizenz: andere | Лицензия: другие | License: others

ERDGASFÖRDERUNG UND -VERBRAUCH
ДОБЫЧА И ПОТРЕБЛЕНИЕ ПРИРОДНОГО ГАЗА
NATURAL GAS PRODUCTION AND CONSUMPTION

36

Billionen Kubikmeter Erdgasreserven besitzt Gazprom
трлн куб. м запасов природного газа владеет Газпром
trillion cubic metres of gas reserves are owned by Gazprom

=

72 %

der Russischen Erdgasreserven
общих запасов российского газа
of the Russian gas reserves

17 %

der globalen Erdgasreserven
мировых запасов газа
of the global gas reserves

420

Milliarden Kubikmeter Erdgas hat Europa 2014 verbraucht
млрд куб.м природного газа Европа использовала в 2014 году
billion cubic metres of natural gas were consumed by Europe in 2014

¼

des Erdgasbedarfs Europas im Jahr 2014 wurden von Gazprom gedeckt
потребности Европы в природном газе в 2014 году поставляет Газпром
of Europe's natural gas demand in 2014 was met by Gazprom

3670

Rubel zahlten russische Konsumenten für 1.000 Kubikmeter Erdgas im Jahr 2014
Europäische Konsumenten zahlten ungefähr das Dreifache
рублей российские потребители платят за 1 000 куб.м газа в 2014 году
Европейские потребители платят примерно в три раза больше
rouble were the cost for 1,000 cubic metres of natural gas for Russian consumers in 2014
European consumers paid approximately three times more

444

Milliarden Kubikmeter Erdgas hat Gazprom 2014 gefördert
млрд куб.м природного газа добыто Газпромом в 2014 году
billion cubic metres of natural gas were produced by Gazprom in 2014

=

69 %

der Gesamtproduktion in Russland
российского объема добычи газа
of the total production in Russia

12 %

der weltweiten Produktion
всемирного объема добычи газа
of the production worldwide

75 %

des geförderten Erdgases kommt von den westsibirischen Erdgasfeldern
природного газа поступает из месторождениях Западной Сибири
of the extracted gas derives from the gas fields in Western Siberia

38 %

wurden nach Europa exportiert
было экспортировано в Европу
was exported to Europe

51 %

wurden in Russland verkauft
были проданы в России
was sold in Russia

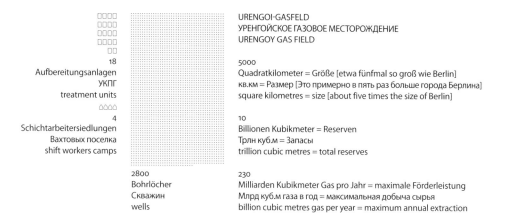

URENGOI-GASFELD
УРЕНГОЙСКОЕ ГАЗОВОЕ МЕСТОРОЖДЕНИЕ
URENGOY GAS FIELD

18
Aufbereitungsanlagen
УКПГ
treatment units

5000
Quadratkilometer = Größe [etwa fünfmal so groß wie Berlin]
кв.км = Размер [Это примерно в пять раз больше города Берлина]
square kilometres = size [about five times the size of Berlin]

4
Schichtarbeitersiedlungen
Вахтовых поселка
shift workers camps

10
Billionen Kubikmeter = Reserven
Трлн куб.м = Запасы
trillion cubic metres = total reserves

2800
Bohrlöcher
Скважин
wells

230
Milliarden Kubikmeter Gas pro Jahr = maximale Förderleistung
Млрд куб.м газа в год = максимальная добыча сырья
billion cubic metres gas per year = maximum annual extraction

PIPELINES NACH WESTEUROPA
ГАЗОПРОВОДЫ В ЗАПАДНУЮ ЕВРОПУ
PIPELINES TO WESTERN EUROPE

Gazprom besitzt das längste Pipelinenetz der Welt mit einer Gesamtlänge von mehr als 170.700 Kilometern.
Das entspricht dem Vierfachen des Erdumfangs.
Компании Газпром принадлежит крупнейшая в мире газотранспортная сеть протяженностью свыше 170 700 километров.
Что соответствует длинне четырех экваторов Земли.
Gazprom owns the longest pipeline network in the world, with a total length of over 170,700 kilometres.
That is equal to four times the circumference of the earth.

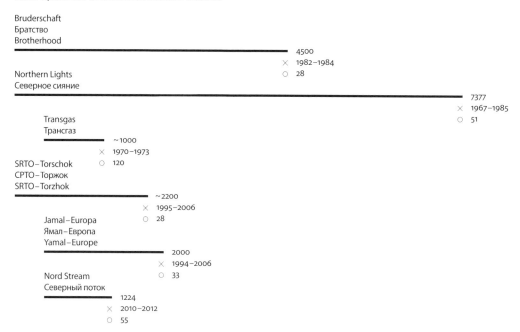

Bruderschaft
Братство
Brotherhood
4500
× 1982–1984
○ 28

Northern Lights
Северное сияние
7377
× 1967–1985
○ 51

Transgas
Трансгаз
~1000
× 1970–1973
○ 120

SRTO–Torschok
СРТО–Торжок
SRTO–Torzhok

~2200
× 1995–2006
○ 28

Jamal–Europa
Ямал–Европа
Yamal–Europe

2000
× 1994–2006
○ 33

Nord Stream
Северный поток
1224
× 2010–2012
○ 55

▬ Länge [km] | Длина [км] | Length [km]
× Errichtung | Строительство | Construction
○ Kapazität [Milliarden m³/Jahr] | Объем [млрд куб.м/год] | Capacity [billion m³/year]

Pipelines
Газопроводы

1

2+3

10

7

9

1   Bruderschaft | Братство | Brotherhood
2   Northern Lights | Северное сияние
3   SRTO–Torschok | СРТО–Торжок | SRTO–Torzhok
4   Jamal–Europa | Ямал–Европа | Yamal–Europe
5   Transgas | Трансгаз
6   Nord Stream | Северный поток
7   Sojus | Союз | Soyuz
8   South Stream | Южный поток [eingestellt | набор | halted]
9   Zentralasien–Zentrum | Средняя Азия–центр | Central Asia–Center
10   Power of Siberia II | Сила Сибири II

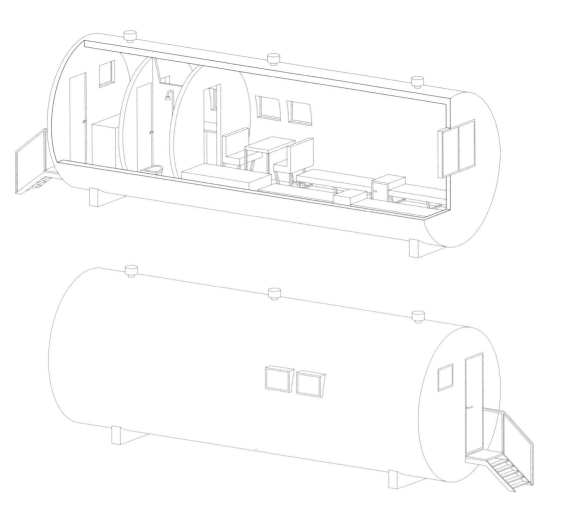

ZEB – Zylindrischer Einheitlicher Bauteil
Das „Fass" wurde Mitte der 1970er Jahre als mobile Unterkunft für
Arbeiter in der Arktis und Subarktis entwickelt.
Eine doppelwandige Stahlplatte bildet die Außenhülle, der runde
Querschnitt ist materialsparend und bietet dem schneidenden
Wind eine geringe Angriffsfläche. Ausstattung für vier Personen:
kleine Küche, WC und Dusche, Sitzecke, vier Betten.

ЦУБ — Цилиндрический Унифицированный Блок
«Бочка» был разработан в середине 1970-х годов в качестве
жилого модуля для работников в Арктике и Субарктике.
Внешняя отделка из листовой стали. Сферическая форма
гарантирует минимальный расход материалов и минимальную
поверхность воздействия резкого ветра. Оборудование для
четырех человек: кухня, туалет и душ, столовая, четыре кровати.

CUB – Cylindrical Unified Component
The 'barrel' was a mobile housing unit developed for workers in
the Arctic and Subarctic in the mid-1970s.
The exterior is a double-layered steel plate. The round cross section
saves building material and reduces the surface exposed to the
piercing winds. Amenities for four people: kitchenette, toilet and
shower, sitting area, four beds.

Glossar
EIN BEITRAG VON GERTRUDE SAXINGER

FERNPENDELN

Diese mobile und flexible Methode zur Bereitstellung von Arbeitskräften für die Erdgasindustrie erklärt sich aus den weiten Entfernungen der Förderanlagen von den Städten. Seit Beginn der Industrialisierung – in der Sowjetunion ab den 1930er Jahren, in Nordwestsibirien seit den 1960er Jahren – wurden große Arbeiterstädte in der Nähe der nördlichen Rohstoffgebiete errichtet, um ein tägliches Pendeln zum Arbeitsplatz zu ermöglichen. Spätestens seit Beginn der 1980er Jahre zeigte sich die Notwendigkeit der Schichtarbeit mit mehrwöchigem Verbleib im Fördergebiet. Grund dafür: Die neu erschlossenen Lagerstätten waren zu weit von den Arbeiterstädten wie z. B. Nowy Urengoi entfernt und nicht durch ein Straßennetz angebunden. Da schon die Erhaltung und die infrastrukturelle Versorgung der vorhandenen inselhaften Städte unter Permafrostbedingungen immer schwieriger wurden – eine arktische Stadt kostet etwa das Vierfache im Vergleich zu einer Stadt in temperierten Zonen – verzichtete man auf Neugründungen.

Heute fernpendeln die Mitarbeiterinnen und Mitarbeiter aus den nördlichen Städten und aus allen Teilen Russlands auf die weit abgeschiedenen Felder. Für einen Zeitraum von mindestens zwei Wochen leben sie dort in Schichtarbeitersiedlungen, um dann für einen ähnlichen Zeitraum zur Erholung nach Hause zurückzukehren. Ein dichtes Netz von Flugverbindungen charakterisiert Nowy Urengoi. Gazprom hat sogar eine eigene Fluglinie für die Belegschaft: Gazpromavia. Viele pendeln jedoch mit dem Zug, was von Moskau bis Nowy Urengoi dreieinhalb Tage in Anspruch nimmt. Aus Kostengründen bezahlen viele Firmen, die mit den Bedingungen eines neoliberalen Weltmarktes mithalten müssen, nur mehr das viel billigere Zugticket. Davon sind vor allem einfache Arbeiterinnen und Arbeiter im Anlagenbausektor betroffen.

FRACHT 200

Die „Erstzugezogenen" planten, nach ein paar Jahren des guten Verdienstes in der Arktis und Subarktis wieder in ihre südliche Heimat zurückzukehren oder sich jedenfalls dort zur letzten Ruhe betten zu lassen. Einen Leichnam aus dem Norden zu überführen nennt man „Fracht 200". In Russland ist die Vorstellung sehr wichtig, dass Verstorbene in der Nähe ihrer Familien beerdigt werden, um in Verbindung mit ihnen bleiben zu können. Allerdings blieben viele im Norden, die sich zuerst nur temporär niederlassen wollten. Daher nahm die Zahl der Überführungen in den letzten Jahren ab, und man lässt sich auf den noch recht kleinen Friedhöfen im Permafrost beerdigen.

Der Begriff „Fracht 200" stammt aus der Militärsprache zur Bezeichnung der Rückführung von Gefallenen. „200" meint hier Kilogramm und bezieht sich auf das Transportgewicht. In sowjetischen Zeiten wurden die Kosten vom Staatsbetrieb übernommen. Im Rahmen der betrieblichen Sozialpakete fördern manche Unternehmen auch heute die „Fracht 200".

GASFACKEL

Steht man auf der prominenten Straßenbrücke im Herzen von Nowy Urengoi und blickt über die Weiten der Stadt oder fährt man durch die polarnächtliche Tundra, leuchten am Horizont die Gasfackeln hoch über den Förderanlagen. Sie sind auch vom Flugzeug aus bei klarem sibirischem Himmel gut sichtbar. Ein beeindruckendes Schauspiel. Für die Menschen im erdöl- und erdgasreichen Norden bedeuten sie mehr als nur das Ablassen von Begleitgasen und das Sicherheitsabfackeln bei Betriebsstörungen oder bei Überdruck in der Anlage. Die stetigen Feuer am Himmel sind ein Zeichen für die pulsierende Industrie, auf die Verlass ist, und dafür, dass das von ihr so stark abhängige Leben seinen gewohnten Gang geht. Das Bild einer Gasfackel findet sich als Symbol der Stadt Nowy Urengoi auf vielen Souvenirs. Eine Attraktion und ein Symbol für Sicherheit im mehrfachen Sinne.

GROSSE ERDE

So werden die Gebiete außerhalb der Siedlungen des Nordens genannt. „Große Erde" ist ein Synonym für Festland, *materik*. Auf der mentalen Landkarte reichen diese nicht nur bis in die dicht besiedelten Regionen Südsibiriens, bis in den kaukasischen Süden oder in den europäischen Teil Russlands, sondern auch bis in die ehemaligen Sowjetrepubliken wie die heutige Ukraine, Moldawien oder nach Kasachstan und in andere zentralasiatische Länder. Die Zugezogenen, aber auch ihre Kinder und Enkel, fühlen sich noch immer mit ihren Herkunftsregionen verbunden. Dort bauen sie Häuser und kaufen Wohnungen, in denen sie die Sommerferien verbringen oder wo sie sich nach der Pensionierung niederlassen wollen. Viele der großen Unternehmen bezahlen ihren Mitarbeiterinnen und Mitarbeitern heute noch, wie schon in sowjetischen

Zeiten, alljährlich oder alle zwei Jahre einen Freiflug auf die Große Erde. „Erde" verweist hier darauf, dass man sich im Norden wie auf einem Trabanten fühlt; der Begriff kann auch mit „Scholle" übersetzt werden, die Erde, in der man verwurzelt ist.

KOLLEKTIV

Die Beschäftigten leben und arbeiten auf engem, weit von städtischem Leben abgeschiedenem Raum. Sozialer Zusammenhalt ist oberste Priorität, wenn lange Polarnächte und sommerliche Dauerhelligkeit, heftige Schnee- und Eisstürme sowie lange Schichten zu enormer Belastung führen. Das Kollektiv der Kolleginnen und Kollegen wird als „zweite Familie" bezeichnet. Nicht nur im russischen Norden, sondern überall in solcherart abgeschlossenen Settings, die typisch für die Erdgas-, Erdöl- und Bergbauindustrie sind, wird dem Individuum hohe Disziplin, Selbstbeherrschung und Empathie abverlangt. Den Schichtarbeiterinnen und Schichtarbeitern wird allgemein nachgesagt, dass es ihnen gelänge, das Gleichgewicht zwischen dem Leben in der Gemeinschaft und ihrem Privatleben zu halten. Vielfach nehmen die Älteren die Jüngeren unter ihre Fittiche und stehen ihnen bei, sich in diesen Lebensstil einzuleben; ganz wie in einer Familie.

KÜCHE

Im Norden, vor allem während der klirrend kalten Monate, trifft man sich zwangsläufig in den Wohnungen. Wie überall in Russland ist auch hier die Küche der beliebteste Treffpunkt. In der sowjetischen Periode waren regelmäßige Restaurantbesuche im Freundeskreis unerschwinglich, weshalb die Küche eine zentrale Rolle im sozialen Leben einnahm – und das ist heute noch so. Man isst Häppchen, trinkt Tee und nimmt ein Schlückchen, während man in vertraulicher Atmosphäre die Sorgen und Freuden des Alltags bespricht. Dieser geschlossene Rahmen ermöglichte es den Familien und ihren Freunden schon in den Zeiten der sowjetischen Repressionen, politische Meinungen gefahrlos austauschen zu können.

Nowy Urengoi kann mit einer soliden Auswahl an Cafés und Restaurants aufwarten. Wenngleich sich das abendliche Ausgehen bei der gut verdienenden Mittelschicht großer Beliebtheit erfreut, sind nach wie vor die eigenen vier Wände der Ort, wo familiäres Beisammensein gelebt wird und die Küche das Zentrum gemeinschaftlicher Gespräche ist.

LANGER RUBEL

Wie in anderen Regionen der Arktis auch, verdienen in Russland die Mitarbeiterinnen und Mitarbeiter des Erdgassektors ein Mehrfaches dessen, was in anderen

Berufen oder in dichter besiedelten Gegenden des Landes gezahlt wird. Aufgrund der nach wie vor sehr niedrigen Löhne in Russland, außerhalb der Zentren Moskau und St. Petersburg, ist der Norden eine beliebte Option, das notwendige Geld für die Ausbildung der Kinder, Wohnraum oder Konsumgüter zu erwirtschaften. Für den „langen Rubel" fernpendeln Menschen oder migrieren langfristig. Vor allem Fachpersonal verdient exzellent. Daher werden Studien an technischen Universitäten bei jungen Menschen immer beliebter, denn gerade für weniger Qualifizierte ist der Wettbewerb um die Arbeitsplätze im Norden sehr hoch. Bereits in der Sowjetunion erstrebte man den „langen Rubel" der Arktis. Allerdings waren vor allem in Zeiten der „Ökonomie der Knappheit" die nichtmonetären Leistungen noch viel attraktiver: man wartete erheblich kürzer auf die Kaufmöglichkeit eines PKWs oder auf die Zuteilung von Wohnraum. Ebenso war die Versorgung mit Gütern des Alltags oder mit Fleisch, Wurst, frischem Gemüse und Obst besser. Die sowjetischen Behörden sicherten sich mit dieser Versorgungspolitik die Motivation der Bürgerinnen und Bürger, in diesen unwirtlichen Gebieten arbeiten zu wollen.

NENZEN

Diese indigene Gruppe, mit einer Größe von etwa 41.000 Personen, gehört zu den letzten Rentiernomaden der Welt. Sie haben den Status der sogenannten „numerisch kleinen Völker des Nordens", was gewisse Rechte mit sich bringt, allerdings keine Landrechte auf das von ihnen bewirtschaftete Gebiet. Während sie 1939 noch 29,3 % der Bevölkerung des nach ihnen benannten Autonomen Kreises der Jamal-Nenzen stellten, waren es aufgrund der massiven Zuwanderung aus dem Süden Russlands, aber auch aufgrund der niedrigen Lebenserwartung der Nenzen, 2010 letztlich nur mehr 5,7 %. Allerdings sind sie seit der von Sowjetrussland betriebenen Politik der Sesshaftmachung in „beiden Welten", der nenzischen und der russischen, gleichermaßen verankert. Im Rahmen der sowjetischen Kollektivierung der Rentierwirtschaft kam es auch zu sozialen Umbrüchen. Kinder wurden in Internatsschulen weit von den Lagern in der Tundra geschickt, an höheren Bildungseinrichtungen ausgebildet und sie erlernten die russische Sprache. Große Teile der nenzischen Bevölkerung leben heute in Siedlungen oder in Städten, auch außerhalb des Nordens.

Wie andere Indigene in der Arktis kämpfen auch die Nenzen mit kulturellem Identitäts- und Sprachverlust, sozialen Problemen und ihrer Unterrepräsentation in der Politik und am Arbeitsmarkt. Graduell fassen sie in der Erdgasindustrie Fuß, werden jedoch auch Opfer der großenteils nicht umweltverträglichen Erdöl- und Erdgasindustrie. Pipelines, Förderanlagen und Industrieschrott durchziehen als Barrieren die Pfade der Tiere, was die Rentierwirtschaft in zunehmendem Maße in Mitleidenschaft zieht. Wenngleich die Firmen zu Kompensationsmaßnahmen verpflichtet sind oder sich im Rahmen von *Corporate Social Responsibility* zu solchen selbst verpflichten, ist die Verhandlungsposition der Nenzen massiv schwächer als jene der Industrie oder der staatlichen Entscheidungsträger, welche die Förderlizenzen vergeben. Prominente Feste, wie der jährliche Tag der Rentierzüchter, werden in den städtischen Zentren ausgerichtet, bei denen mit Kunsthandwerk, Kostümen, Geschichten, Performances und Wettbewerben die indigene Kultur traditionalistisch gefeiert wird. Gleichzeitig sind Internet, Smartphones und Videospiele auch in den entlegenen Nomadenzelten der Tundra angekommen.

120 ## NORDBEWOHNER
Diese umgangssprachliche Selbstbezeichnung der in den letzten Jahrzehnten in die Industriestädte der Arktis und Subarktis zugezogenen Bevölkerung verwenden die Leute vor allem dann, wenn sie das „Besondere" ihrer Lebensweise hervorheben wollen. Sie verweisen auf ihre schwierige körperliche und psychische Adaptierung an die klimatischen und landschaftlichen Verhältnisse und sind sehr stolz darauf, sie bewältigt zu haben. Die dort geborenen Kinder werden als „Nordbewohner" sozialisiert und somit wird die Idee des Besonderen weitergegeben. Man verweist auf den starken Zusammenhalt der Menschen und die gegenseitige Unterstützung auch zwischen Fremden, um die Unbill der Region meistern zu können: „Wenn man mit dem Auto am Straßenrand liegen bleibt, wird niemand vorbeifahren, sondern man wird stets gefragt werden, wie einem geholfen werden könne. Wir lassen uns bei minus 40 Grad Celsius nicht im Stich."

PIONIERE
Viele Industriestädte im Norden und in Sibirien wurden ab den 1930er Jahren unter Stalin durch Zwangsarbeit im Rahmen des Gulag-Systems errichtet. Ab der Tauwetterperiode in den 1950er Jahren unter Nikita Chruschtschow suchte man dann andere Möglichkeiten, den enormen Arbeitskräftebedarf für den Aufbau der Städte und der Industrie abzudecken. Menschen wurden vor allem über die Verteilungsprogramme für Universitätsabgänger, *raspredelenie*, und über die Jugendorganisation der KPdSU, *komsomolskaja putjowka*, rekrutiert. Diese Arbeiter nannten sich Pioniere oder „Erstzugezogene", *perwoprochodzy*. Man verstand es als große patriotische Ehre, für die politisch

und wirtschaftlich so wichtige Aufgabe, den Norden zu „zivilisieren" und ihn als städtischen Lebensraum zu entwickeln, ausgewählt zu werden – er sicherte durch seine reichen Rohstoffvorkommen den Staatshaushalt der Sowjetunion. Zu Beginn wohnten die Zugezogenen in Zelten oder in „Fässer" genannten Containern, russisch *botschka*, dann in Holzhäusern. Später wurde ihnen Wohnraum in den Plattenbauten zugeteilt. Vollständig abgeschlossen ist die Umsiedlung in die Hochhäuser noch immer nicht. Heute verweisen Denkmäler und Straßennamen auf die Errungenschaften dieser Generation.

SCHICHTARBEITERSIEDLUNG
Sie befinden sich in geringer, aber sicherer Entfernung von den Förderanlagen und sind im besten Falle mit Bussen, in den meist schwierigeren Fällen nur mit der *Wachtowka*, einem schweren LKW mit Passagierkabine, oder mit dem Helikopter erreichbar. Die Belegschaften wohnen dort jeweils für mehrere Wochen in Modulen funktionaler Bauweise oder in mobilen Containerdörfern. Die Größen variieren zwischen mehreren tausend und nur ein paar Dutzend Menschen, je nach Arbeitskräftebedarf in den unterschiedlichen Typen von Anlagen und Baustellen. Stationäre Camps zeichnen sich meist durch eine Infrastruktur aus, in der für das Wohlbefinden der Mitarbeiterinnen und Mitarbeiter so gut wie möglich gesorgt wird.

Der monotone Zyklus von Kantinenessen, Arbeiten, Schlafen kann zu hoher psychischer und physischer Belastung führen, insbesondere wenn eine Schicht länger als einen Monat dauert. Während die großen, oftmals staatsnahen Betriebe ihr Bestes für den Erhalt der Zufriedenheit ihrer Mitarbeiterinnen und Mitarbeiter geben, wird kleineren, privaten Subunternehmen nachgesagt, dass hygienische Standards und die Unterbringung oft stark zu wünschen übrig lassen.

In den Siedlungen leben die Menschen unter Kontrolle der Firma. Der Tagesablauf ist strikt getaktet und das Verlassen der Anlage in der Freizeit, mehrheitlich aus Gründen der Sicherheit, untersagt. Üblicherweise herrscht Alkoholverbot, um soziale Spannungen bei der eng zusammenlebenden Belegschaft zu vermeiden. Illegaler Konsum ist die Konsequenz. Um sich zusätzliche Kontrollen zu ersparen, erlauben manche Unternehmen moderates Trinken. Es werden jedoch unangekündigte Alkohol- und Drogentests durchgeführt, um Sicherheitsprobleme an den gefährlichen Arbeitsplätzen zu verhindern. Die Mitarbeiterinnen und Mitarbeiter stimmen dieser Überwachung im Rahmen ihres Arbeitsvertrages zu. Mehrmalige Verletzung der Regeln wird mit Entlassung geahndet.

SOZIALPAKET

So werden umfangreiche betriebliche Sozialleistungen für Mitarbeiterinnen und Mitarbeiter bezeichnet. Diese reichen von vergünstigten Sanatoriums- und Urlaubsaufenthalten, medizinischer Zusatzversicherung, Universitätsstipendien für die Kinder der Angestellten bis hin zu gefördertem Wohnraum auf der Großen Erde, meist in den südlichen Zentralregionen. Diese geförderten Immobilien, z. B. in Moskau, St. Petersburg oder in den regionalen Hauptstädten, sind eine vielversprechende Wertanlage.

STADTBILDENDER BETRIEB

Ähnlich wie die landwirtschaftlichen Kolchosen und Sowchosen waren auch andere Betriebe und sogenannte Kombinate in der Sowjetunion nicht nur für die eigentliche Produktion zuständig oder der Hauptarbeitgeber einer Stadt. Sie organisierten darüber hinaus die technische und soziale Infrastruktur, unterhielten somit Einrichtungen wie Schulen und Kindergärten, Kinos oder Geschäfte und waren auch für Wohnungs- und Straßenbau zuständig. Ganz anders stellt sich die Situation in der Russischen Föderation dar, in der die zentralen Versorgungsaufgaben an die Munizipalitäten übertragen und andere Bereiche privatisiert wurden. So auch in den arktischen und subarktischen Industriestädten. Allerdings erscheint der rohstoffreiche Norden in dieser Hinsicht noch immer als Spezifikum mit sowjetischen Reminiszenzen. Denn im Vergleich zu anderen Landesteilen werden im Norden nur relativ langsam, man könnte auch sagen „behutsam", die nicht zum Kernprofil der rohstofffördernden Unternehmen gehörenden Teile ausgegliedert oder privatisiert.

Der stadtbildende Betrieb in Nowy Urengoi ist der Gazprom-Konzern mit seinen lokalen Tochterunternehmen. Er ist für gute Gehälter und umfangreiche betriebliche Sozialleistungen (siehe „Sozialpaket") bekannt. Neue, nicht staatsnahe Arbeitgeber operieren innerhalb eines international marktüblichen, finanziell eng geschnürten Korsetts und bieten den Mitarbeiterinnen und Mitarbeitern daher weniger. Der Unmut über den Verlust von Privilegien ist bei Angestellten von privaten Firmen natürlich groß, vor allem die Älteren unter ihnen fühlen sich um die „Entschädigung" für ihre Leistungen zum Aufbau dieser Industrieregionen unter klimatisch harschen Bedingungen betrogen. Somit ist die Realität, die der Umbau eines Wirtschaftssystems mit sich bringt, im Norden Russlands, wenn auch recht spät, angekommen. Dennoch steht das größte Unternehmen einer monoindustriellen Stadt symbolisch und als Arbeitgeber im Zentrum des Lebens ihrer Bevölkerung. Die Menschen sind ihm gegenüber höchst loyal, erwarten sich jedoch sozialen Schutz und wirtschaftliche Stabilität.

Unter dem Titel *Corporate Social Responsibility* vermitteln die Großbetriebe heute ihr Engagement für den Erhalt einer lebenswerten Stadt. In Nowy Urengoi reicht dies vom Sport- und Kulturzentrum von Gazprom bis hin zur Ausrichtung von Festen oder der Unterstützung von Sozialprojekten.

TRINKSPRUCH

Mit „Auf uns, auf Euch, auf Öl und Gas!" prostet man sich in den Erdöl- und Erdgasregionen gerne zu. Neben den vielen Liedern, Sprichwörtern und Gedichten, die über die Natur, die reich vorhandenen Rohstoffe, die Stadt oder die prägenden Unternehmen im Norden zu hören sind, gehört dieser Toast zum Ausdruck eines Lebensgefühls. Die schwer arbeitenden, den Herausforderungen der Arktis trotzenden Menschen haben den Rohstoff, der sie „ernährt", regelrecht lieb gewonnen. Sie sind sich dessen bewusst, dass sie ohne Erdöl und Erdgas nicht hier wären.

Словарь терминов
КОММЕНТАРИИ ГЕРТРУДЕ ЗАКСИНГЕР

БОЛЬШАЯ ЗЕМЛЯ

Так называются территории, не относящиеся к Северным посёлкам. Большая земля — синоним материка. Если мы представим себе карту, то она охватит районы от Южной Сибири до Кавказа, европейскую часть России и даже такие бывшие советские республики как Украину, Молдавию или Казахстан и другие центральноазиатские страны. Северные переселенцы, их дети и внуки чувствуют связь со своей материковой родиной: они строят там дома и покупают квартиры, проводят в них каникулы или планируют перебраться туда после выхода на пенсию. Многие крупные предприятия и сегодня, как и в советские времена, оплачивают своим работникам ежегодно или раз в два года перелёты на Большую землю. «Земля» означает здесь, что человек чувствует себя на севере, как на Луне; это понятие можно перевести как «родной клочок земли», где остались твои корни.

ВАХТОВЫЙ МЕТОД

Этот мобильный и гибкий метод обеспечивает рабочую силу для газовой отрасли, он возник из-за большой удалённости мест разработок. С началом индустриализации в 1930-х годах (в северо-западной Сибири этот процесс пришёлся на 60-е годы), в СССР началось строительство больших промышленных городов неподалёку от залежей полезных ископаемых, чтобы перевозить рабочих ежедневно к месту работы. С начала 80-х годов появилась необходимость оставлять рабочих на трудовой вахте по нескольку недель. Причиной стали разработки новых месторождений, которые находились далеко от таких городов, таких как Новый Уренгой — между ними не было ещё дорожного сообщения. Поддерживать необходимое жизнеобеспечение города-острова в вечной мерзлоте становилось все труднее и дороже (один арктический город стоит почти в четыре раза дороже города в умеренной климатической зоне), поэтому было решено отказаться от постройки новых городов.

Сегодня сотрудники ездят из северных городов и всех уголков России на отдалённые места разработок. Вахтовый метод основан на принципе минимум две недели работы — две недели отдыха дома. Новый Уренгой располагает хорошим воздушным сообщением. Газпром даже проложил воздушный маршрут для своих работников — Газпромавиа.

Однако многие курсируют поездом, который идёт из Москвы до Нового Уренгоя три с половиной дня. Чтобы соответствовать условиям неолиберального мирового рынка, многие фирмы оплачивают своим работникам дешёвые железнодорожные билеты. В основном это касается простых рабочих, занятых на монтажных работах.

ВАХТОВЫЙ ПОСЁЛОК

Они расположены на безопасном расстоянии, но недалеко от мест добычи и туда можно добраться в лучшем случае автобусом, в основном же вахтовкой — грузовиком с пассажирской кабиной — или же вертолётом. Рабочие живут там в течение нескольких недель в жилых модулях или в так называемых деревнях, образованных из мобильных контейнеров. Население такой деревни варьируется от нескольких тысяч человек до нескольких десятков, в зависимости от количества рабочих, занятых на различных типах оборудования и строительных площадках. Стационарные лагеря в основном хорошо благоустроены и как можно лучше соответствуют потребностям работников.

Монотонный цикл жизни: столовая — работа — сон может вызвать сильное психическое и физическое перенапряжение, особенно, если вахта длится более одного месяца. В то время как большие, чаще государственные, предприятия предлагают наилучшие условия для удовлетворения потребностей своих работников, малые частные предприятия, по слухам, оставляют желать лучшего в отношении жилья и санитарных условий.

Жизнь в посёлках контролируется фирмой: действует строгий распорядок дня, к тому же в свободное время, большей частью в целях безопасности, запрещено покидать территорию. Почти повсеместно введён запрет на алкоголь, дабы избежать социального напряжения между работниками, которые вынуждены долгое время проживать в тесном контакте. Как следствие — подпольное употребление алкоголя. Чтобы избежать частых проверок, некоторые предприятия разрешили своим работникам употреблять ограниченное количество спиртного. Внезапные проверки на алкогольное и наркотическое опьянение призваны повысить безопасность сотрудников на опасных рабочих местах. Подписывая трудовой договор, работники соглашаются на прохождение этого контроля. Повторное нарушение правил ведёт к увольнению.

ГРАДООБРАЗУЮЩЕЕ ПРЕДПРИЯТИЕ

Подобно сельскохозяйственным колхозам и совхозам, другие предприятия и так называемые комбинаты занимались не только производством основного продукта и являлись не только основными работодателями в городе. Они организовывали техническую и социальную инфраструктуру, открывали школы, детские сады, кинотеатры и магазины, а также занимались строительством жилья и дорог. Совсем иная картина сложилась в Российской Федерации, где основные задачи коммунального обеспечения переданы муниципалитетам, а другие области приватизированы. Так же обстоят дела и в арктических и субарктических промышленных городах. Тем не менее, богатый природными ресурсами Север имеет всё ещё особый статус и является осколком СССР. Здесь, по сравнению с другими районами страны, приватизация активов, которые не принадлежат к главному профилю предприятий, проводится очень медленно, можно сказать осторожно.

Градообразующее предприятие Нового Уренгоя Газпром, со своими дочерними предприятиями, славится хорошими зарплатами и разнообразными льготами (см. Соцпакет). Новые негосударственные предприятия-работодатели функционируют в рамках международного рынка, несколько стеснены в финансировании и предлагают своим работникам меньшую оплату. Работники частных фирм, прежде всего старшего поколения, испытывают большое недовольство от потери привилегий. Они недовольны компенсацией за свои усилия по освоению и индустриализации региона с суровыми климатическими условиями и чувствуют себя обманутыми. Таким образом, последствия изменения экономической системы, хоть и позже, но пришли на российский Север. И всё-таки самое большое предприятие монопромышленного города является центром жизни горожан. Люди демонстрируют высокую приверженность своему предприятию и ожидают от него социальной защиты и экономической стабильности.

Под девизом «корпоративной социальной ответственности», крупные предприятия заботятся о благоустройстве города, что подтверждается многочисленными примерами, начиная от спортивного и культурного центра Газпрома и заканчивая проведением праздников и поддержкой социальных проектов.

ГРУЗ 200

«Первопроходцы» планировали через пару лет хороших заработков в Арктике и Субарктике возвратиться на Родину или найти там свой последний приют. Переправка тела с Севера называется «Груз 200». В России широко распространено представление, что покойные должны быть похоронены рядом с местом проживания своих семей, чтобы оставаться на связи с ними. Тем не менее, многие, приехавшие на время, остаются на Севере навсегда, в результате число таких перевозок в последние годы сократилось, поэтому умерших теперь хоронят на маленьких кладбищах в вечной мерзлоте.

Термин «Груз 200» пришёл из военной лексики и обозначает возвращение павших на Родину. 200 килограммов — транспортируемый вес. В советские времена перевозка оплачивалась государством. Некоторые предприятия и сегодня предлагают своим сотрудникам социальный пакет, куда входит также перевозка «Груза 200».

ДЛИННЫЙ РУБЛЬ

Как и в других регионах Арктики, работники газовой отрасли в России зарабатывают во много раз больше тех, кто работает в других профессиях или на плотно заселенных территориях. По причине всё ещё очень низких зарплат в России, кроме Москвы и Петербурга, Север является популярной возможностью, чтобы заработать деньги, необходимые на образование детей, покупку квартиры или потребительских товаров. В погоне за «длинным рублём» людям приходится переселяться на долгое время или постоянно преодолевать огромные расстояния, курсируя между работой и домом. Отлично зарабатывают, в первую очередь, специалисты. Поэтому учеба на технических факультетах пользуется большим спросом у молодёжи, потому что среди неквалифицированных работников конкуренция за рабочие места особенно высока. Уже в СССР люди устремлялись в Арктику за «длинным рублём». Хотя как раз во времена дефицита неденежные блага были наиболее привлекательны: возможность покупки машины или получение квартиры вне очереди. На Севере гораздо лучше было организовано снабжение товарами народного потребления и продуктами питания: мясом, колбасой, свежими овощами и фруктами. Таким образом советское правительство обеспечивало интерес граждан к работе в суровых климатических условиях.

КОЛЛЕКТИВ

Работники живут и работают в узком кругу, вдалеке от городской жизни, в замкнутом пространстве. Социальная сплочённость является главным приоритетом, потому что полярная ночь, полярный день, снежные бури, а также длинные рабочие смены ведут к экстремальной нагрузке. Коллектив сотрудников называют «второй семьёй». Не только на российском

Севере, но и повсюду, где люди работают в подобных условиях, типичных для нефтегазовой отрасли и горнодобывающей промышленности, от человека требуется высокая дисциплина, самообладание и сопереживание. Говорят, вахтовикам удаётся соблюдать баланс между коллективной и частной жизнью. Старшие берут под своё крыло младших и помогают им обосноваться в этой жизни; совсем как в семье.

КУХНЯ

На севере, в трескучие морозные месяцы, собраться вместе можно только в квартирах. Как и повсюду в России, кухня является излюбленным местом встреч. Постоянные встречи с друзьями в ресторане были в советский период недоступны, поэтому кухня приобрела центральную роль в социальной жизни, это справедливо и для сегодняшних реалий. В доверительной атмосфере, за чаем с бутербродами, опрокидывая стопку, люди делятся своими печалями и радостями. Ещё в репрессивные советские времена, в узком кругу своей семьи и друзей люди могли безопасно вести разговоры о политике.

Новый Уренгой располагает солидным выбором ресторанов и кафе. Хотя вечернее посещение ресторанов пользуется популярностью среди состоятельного среднего класса, кухня, как и прежде, является центром семейных посиделок.

НЕНЦЫ

Ненцы принадлежат к группе коренных народов Севера, их насчитывается примерно 41 000 человек и они являются последними в мире кочевниками-оленеводами. Ненцам присвоен статус «малочисленных народов крайнего Севера», что подразумевает некоторые преимущества, однако не даёт прав на землю, где расположены их пастбища. Если 1939 году Ямало-Ненецкий автономный округ насчитывал 29,3 % коренного населения, то к 2010-му году всего лишь 5,7 %, в связи с массовыми переселениями с юга России, но также по причине низкой продолжительности жизни ненцев. Советский Союз проводил политику оседлости среди ненцев, в результате этот народ укоренился в двух культурах: собственно ненецкой и русской. Во времена советской коллективизации, социальные потрясения не обошли стороной и оленеводство. Дети учились в школах-интернатах, далеко от стойбищ в тундре, изучали русский язык, получали высшее образование. Много ненцев живут сегодня в посёлках и городах на Большой Земле.

Как и другие коренные народы Арктики, ненцы борются за свою культурную идентичность, против потери языка. Они преодолевают социальные

проблемы: среди политиков очень мало представителей ненецкого народа, безработица среди ненцев довольно высока. Ненцы постепенно приходят и в газовую отрасль, в тоже время они являются её жертвами, потому что промышленная добыча не благоприятствует сохранению экологического баланса. Трубопроводы, буровые установки и индустриальный металлолом встают барьером на оленьих тропах, отчего оленеводство всё больше страдает. Хотя многие фирмы и обязаны возмещать ущерб оленеводам или сами наложили на себя такое обязательство в рамках «корпоративный социальной ответственности», вес ненцев в спорных вопросах намного слабее позиции чиновников и представителей отрасли, получивших от государства лицензию на производство работ. Важные праздники, такие как День оленевода, проводятся в городских центрах, они стали традиционными праздниками этого коренного народа, ненцы проводят состязания на ловкость, конкурсы декоративно-прикладных ремесел и костюмов, рассказывают легенды и показывают различные представления. Вместе с тем интернет, смартфоны и видеоигры проникли даже в самые отдаленные чумы кочевников, разбросанные по тундре.

ПИОНЕРЫ

Многие из промышленных городов Севера и Сибири были построены в 1930-х годах при Сталине. На строительстве использовался принудительный труд заключённых ГУЛАГа. Начиная с хрущёвской оттепели в 1950-х годах властям пришлось искать другие возможности, чтобы обеспечить достаточное количество рабочей силы для строительства городов и развития промышленности. В основном туда поехали по распределению выпускники университетов и комсомольцы, по комсомольским путёвкам. Они называли себя пионерами или первопроходцами. Считалось большой честью быть выбранными для решения таких грандиозных политических и экономических задач как освоение Сибири, благодаря богатым природным ресурсам обеспечивался государственный бюджет СССР. Сначала рабочие жили в палатках и так называемых «бочках» — контейнерах, а потом и в деревянных домах. Позже людей стали расселять в квартиры в панельных домах. Процесс переселения в высотные дома всё ещё не завершен. Памятники и названия улиц напоминают нам сегодня о достижениях этого поколения.

СЕВЕРНЫЙ ЧЕЛОВЕК

Так стали называть себя в последние десятилетия люди, переехавшие жить и работать в промышленные города Арктики. Это название употребляется в разговорной речи, по большей части когда люди хотят подчеркнуть «особенность» устройства их жизни. Они подчеркивают тяжёлые физические и психические нагрузки, суровые климатические и природные условия, и очень гордятся тем, что смогли их преодолеть. Рождённые на Севере дети воспитываются как «северные люди», в результате чего эта идея особенности передаётся из поколения в поколение. Даже в отношениях между чужими людьми отмечается крепкая сплочённость и взаимовыручка. Это необходимо, чтобы освоиться в трудном регионе: «Если машина стоит на обочине, никто не проедет мимо, все будут останавливаться и спрашивать, могут ли они чем-нибудь помочь. Мы не оставляем друг друга в беде при сорокаградусном морозе».

СОЦПАКЕТ

Так называются всевозможные социальные льготы для работников: начиная от санаториев и баз отдыха, дополнительных медицинских услуг, университетских стипендий для детей сотрудников и заканчивая значительными субсидиями на жильё на Большой земле, чаще всего в южных регионах страны. Полученная на таких льготных основаниях недвижимость в Москве, Петербурге или в региональных центрах считается перспективным вложением средств.

ТОСТ

Со словами: «За нас, за вас, за нефть и газ!» люди охотно поднимают тост в нефте- и газодобывающих регионах. Наряду с песнями, пословицами и стихами, повествующими о природе и её богатствах, о городе и его знаменитых предприятиях, этот тост выражает особенное жизнеощущение северян. Несмотря на тяжелую работу и преодоление суровых условий Арктики, люди полюбили недра земли, которые их кормят. Они сознают, что без открытия нефтегазовых месторождений их бы тут не было.

ФАКЕЛ

Если встать на знаменитом городском мосту в сердце Нового Уренгоя и вглядеться в городские просторы, или же проехаться по тундре в полярную ночь, то на горизонте можно увидеть газовые факелы, высоко пылающие над месторождениями. В ясном сибирском небе они хорошо видны — впечатляющий спектакль! Для людей Севера, богатого нефтью и газом, эти факелы значат больше, чем простое сжигание попутного газа в целях безопасности при сбоях в производстве или в случае избыточного давления в системе. Постоянные факелы в небе — знак пульсирующей индустрии, которая даёт надёжность

и позволяет жизни, так зависимой от неё, идти своим чередом.

Изображение газового факела является символом Нового Уренгоя, его можно увидеть на многих сувенирах. Этот огонь стал достопримечательностью и символом стабильности, во многих смыслах.

Glossary
BY GERTRUDE SAXINGER

BIG EARTH

This term refers to the regions outside the settlements of the North. 'Big Earth' is a synonym for the mainland, *materik*. On the mental map these regions extend not only to the densely populated areas of Southern Siberia, to the Caucasian South or to the European parts of Russia, but also to the former Soviet republics, like Moldova or today's Ukraine, and even to Kazakhstan or other countries in Central Asia. The new settlers, and their children and grandchildren, too, still feel attached to their regions of origin. It's where they build homes and buy apartments, where they spend their summer holidays or where they settle down after retirement. Today, as in Soviet times, many of the large companies pay for a plane ticket to the Big Earth for their employees once every year or two years. The term 'earth' points to the fact that the settlers of the North feel like living on a satellite. The term can also be translated as 'clod', meaning the soil one is firmly rooted in.

CARGO 200

The first residents arriving in the North had planned to return to their southern homes or at least to be laid to rest there after several years of good earnings in the Arctic or Subarctic. The transfer of a body is commonly called 'Cargo 200'. In Russia, the idea of being buried close to the family so that one may stay connected is very important. However, many workers remained in the North despite initially intending to stay only temporarily. So the number of transfers of bodies has declined steadily in recent years, and people now choose to be buried in the as yet small cemeteries in the permafrost.

'Cargo 200' is originally a military term and describes the transfer of soldiers killed in action. The number '200' refers to the transport weight in kilograms. In Soviet times, the costs for transporting mortal remains home were borne by the state-owned businesses. Today, some companies include 'Cargo 200' in their employee benefits packages.

CITY-FORMING ENTERPRISE

Like the agricultural kolkhozes and sovkhozes, other enterprises and combines in the Soviet Union were not only responsible for the actual production and for being the principal employer in the city. In addition, they organised the technical and social infrastructure. They maintained all institutions, such as schools and kindergartens. They were responsible for cinemas, shops, housing, and road construction. However, the situation in the Russian Federation is quite different. The central supply obligations were transferred to the municipalities and other sectors were privatised. The Arctic and Subarctic industrial cities are no exception. However, the North, rich in resources as it is, appears as a specific that is reminiscent of the situation in the Soviet Union. Here, the business units that do not belong to the core sector of the extracting industries are outsourced or privatised only gradually – one could also say, gently – compared to other parts of Russia.

The city-forming enterprise in Novy Urengoy is the Gazprom Corporation with its local subsidiary companies. It is renowned for its good wages and its comprehensive social employee benefits (see 'social package'). New companies that don't have such close ties to the state have to operate within a close financial framework that is customary in the international markets, thus offer less to their employees. Naturally, there is great resentment among the employees of private companies about having lost their privileges. Particularly the older employees feel cheated out of their 'compensation' for their efforts in building up these industrial regions under such harsh climatic conditions. Thus the ramifications of the transformation of the economic system are felt in Russia's North, too, albeit delayed. Nevertheless, as the main employer in a mono-industrial city the biggest company stands at the centre of the life of its inhabitants, both economically and symbolically. The residents are highly loyal towards the company, but they expect social protection and economic stability in return.

Under the banner of Corporate Social Responsibility the big companies convey their commitment to building a city worth living in. In Novy Urengoy, Gazprom funds a cultural and sports centre, organises festivals, and supports social projects.

COLLECTIVE GROUP

The employees live and work in cramped conditions, far away from urban life. Social cohesion is a top priority when endless polar nights in winter or constant daylight in summer, violent blizzards or ice storms, and strenuous work shifts put enormous pressure on the employees. The collective of the colleagues functions as a 'second family'. The conditions in the secluded settings that characterise the oil, gas, and mining industry, not only in the Russian North, but elsewhere in the world, too, demand a high degree of discipline, self-restraint, and empathy. Generally, the workers are said to succeed in keeping the balance between life in the community and their private life. Commonly, the older people take the younger ones under their wing and support them in settling into this rough life, just like in a family.

FLARE STACK

Standing on the prominent road bridge in the heart of Novy Urengoy with a view over the city or driving through the night of the polar tundra, one can see the gas flares shine on the horizon high above the gas production installations. They are also visible from an airplane, if the Siberian sky is clear. It is an impressive sight. To the people in the oil and gas rich regions of the North, the flares mean more than just the discharge of associated gases or flaring in case of an operational breakdown or overpressure in the system. The steady fires in the sky signify a vibrant industry that can be relied upon. They show that their life, which is so dependent on the flourishing of this industry, will continue as usual. The image of a flare stack can be found on many souvenirs as a symbol of Novy Urengoy. They are an attraction and a symbol of security in many senses.

KITCHEN

In the North, particularly in the biting cold winter, people are forced to socialise in their homes. As everywhere in Russia, here too the eat-in kitchen is the most popular meeting place. During Soviet times, eating out at a restaurant with friends was prohibitively expensive, so the kitchen played a key role in social life, and this continues until today. You have some snacks, drink a cup of tea or take a sip of something stronger, and talk about the sorrows and joys of daily life in private, familiar surroundings. This goes back to the times of Soviet repression, when the intimate, private setting made it possible for families and friends to safely exchange their political views.

Novy Urengoy boasts a decent range of restaurants and cafés. Although going out in the evening with friends enjoys great popularity among middle-class families with a good income, the home is still the place for a family-style gathering, and the kitchen is the heart of the conversations.

LONG-DISTANCE COMMUTING

This mobile and flexible method of supplying the necessary workforce for the natural gas industry can be explained by the long distances between the gas production plants and the residential towns. Since the beginning of industrialisation – 1930s in the Soviet Union, 1960s in northwest Siberia – big cities were built close to the northern sites of resources. Thus, the workers were able to commute to their workplaces every day. In the early 1980s it became necessary that the workers stayed in the extraction areas for shifts lasting several weeks, because the newly developed deposits were too far removed from the residential towns such as Novy Urengoy and were not connected to the road network. As infrastructure maintenance and the supply of the existing island-like cities under permafrost conditions became more and more difficult – a city in the Arctic is four times more expensive than a city in temperate zones – establishing new cities wasn't considered feasible.

Today, workers commute long-distance from the cities in the North and from all parts of Russia to the faraway, secluded gas fields. For a period of at least two weeks they live in their shift workers accommodation, and then they return home for a similar period of time for recreation. Novy Urengoy has a dense air travel network. Gazprom even has its own airline for its workers: Gazpromavia. However, many workers commute by train. The journey from Moscow to Novy Urengoy takes three and a half days. Due to the cost factor, many companies that have to keep up with the demands of a neoliberal world economy only pay for the much cheaper train ticket. This mainly affects ordinary workers that work in the construction of facilities and installation.

LONG ROUBLE

Like in other Arctic regions, the Russian employees in the natural gas sector earn a multiple of what is paid in other professions or in more densely populated areas of Russia. Because of the still-low wages that are paid in Russia outside the centres Moscow and St. Petersburg, the North is a popular option of earning the money necessary for children's education, purchasing a home, or for consumer goods. As a result, people commute long distances or migrate for long periods for the 'long rouble'. Well-trained specialists in particular earn very high salaries. Thus, studying at a technical university is becoming an increasingly popular option for young people, particularly as the competition for employment in the North is very high for less qualified workers. The 'long rouble' of the Arctic was already highly sought-after in the Soviet Union. However, particularly in times of the 'economy of scarcity', non-monetary benefits were even more attractive: these benefits included considerably shorter waiting times for buying a car or the allocation of accommodation. Equally, the supply with everyday goods, meat, fresh vegetables, and fruit was much better. Soviet government agencies used this supply policy to ensure there was enough motivation to work in inhospitable areas.

NENETS

This indigenous ethnic group comprises approximately 41,000 people and is one of the last peoples of reindeer nomads in the world. They have been given the status of the so-called 'numerically small peoples of the North'. That status entails certain rights, although it doesn't include land rights in the area where they live and which they cultivate. In 1939, the Nenets accounted for 29.3 % of the population in the Yamalo-Nenets Autonomous Okrug, which is named after them. But in 2010, this figure had decreased to only 5.7 % due to mass immigration from southern Russia and their low life expectancy. However, as a result of Soviet settlement policy the Nenets are at home in both worlds, the Nenets one and the Russian one. The collectivisation of reindeer husbandry under the Soviets led to drastic social changes. The children of the Nenets were sent to boarding schools, far away from their settlements in the tundra. They were trained at higher educational institutions and had to learn the Russian language. Today, large sections of the Nenets population live in settlements or towns, sometimes outside the North.

Like other indigenous people in the Arctic, the Nenets too are struggling with the loss of their cultural identity and their language, with social problems, and with their under-representation in politics and in the labour market. Gradually, they are gaining ground in the natural gas industry, but they often become victims of the mostly noxious oil and gas industry, too. Pipelines, production plants, and industrial waste obstruct the migration paths of the animals, which increasingly affects reindeer husbandry. Although the gas and oil companies are obligated to provide compensatory measures or have committed to such measures under the principles of Corporate Social Responsibility, the negotiation position of the Nenets is much weaker than that of the industry or the government decision makers that issue the exploration licences. The urban centres play host to popular traditional festivals, like the annual Reindeer Breeders' Day, which celebrates indigenous culture in a traditional way with games, crafts, traditional costumes, tales, and performances. At the same time, the internet, smartphones, and video games have arrived even in the remotest of remote nomad tents in the tundra.

NORTHERNER

This colloquial self-designation of the people who have moved to the industrial cities of the Arctic or the Subarctic in the past decades is used particularly when people want to emphasise the exceptional circumstances of their way of life. They stress how difficult it is to physically and mentally adapt to the climatic and natural conditions and they are immensely proud to have mastered them. The children who are born in the area are socialised as 'Northerners' and so this notion of distinctiveness is passed on. The term also refers to the strong social cohesion and the mutual help and assistance even among strangers, which is needed in order to deal with the hardships of Arctic life: 'When your car breaks down, absolutely nobody will drive past – people will always ask how they can help. At 40 degrees below zero, we don't leave anyone stranded.'

PIONEERS

Beginning in the 1930s under Stalin, many industrial towns in the North and in Siberia were built using forced labour of Gulag prisoners. From the Khrushchev thaw in the 1950s onwards, other options for meeting the enormous need for labour for building the towns and the industry were being explored. The workers were now mostly recruited by way of distribution schemes for university graduates, *razpredelenie*, or by the youth organisation of the CPSU, *komsomolskaya putevka*. These workers called themselves pioneers or first settlers, *pervoprokhodtsy*. They considered it a great patriotic honour to be chosen for the politically and economically important task of 'civilising' the North and developing urban environments there, for the abundance of natural resources of the North secured the national budget of the Soviet Union. In the beginning, the settlers lived in tents or in containers, so-called 'barrels', *botshka*, later in wooden huts. Eventually they would be allocated an apartment in a prefabricated high-rise. The relocation into these apartements has not yet been completed. Today, memorials and street names commemorate the achievements of the first generation of settlers.

SHIFT WORKERS CAMP

The camps are located at a short, but safe distance from the gas treatment units. In the best cases, they can be reached by bus. However, mostly they are more difficult to reach, and the workers have to use a *vakhtovka* – a heavy lorry with a passenger cabin –, or a helicopter. The workers stay in the camps for several weeks. They live in functional modules or mobile container villages. The size of these villages varies between several thousand inhabitants and just a few dozen,

128

depending on the labour requirements of the different types of plants or construction sites. Stationary camps are usually characterised by an infrastructure that ensures the comfort and well-being of the workers as much as possible.

The monotonous routine of eating in the canteen, working, and sleeping can result in significant physical and mental stress, particularly when the duration of the shift exceeds one month. Whereas the large companies that have close ties to the government do their best to ensure the satisfaction of the workers, it is said of the small private subcontractors that the standards of hygiene and living conditions leave much to be desired.

In the camps, people's lives are controlled by the company. Their days are strictly regulated. It is prohibited to leave the compound during free time, primarily for security reasons. Generally, alcohol is strictly prohibited in order to prevent social tensions between the workers, who live together in such confined spaces. The consequence is illegal consumption of alcohol. In order to avoid having to conduct additional checks, some companies allow moderate drinking, using spot checks for drug or alcohol use to try to prevent security problems at work. The workers have agreed to this level of control in their employment contracts. Repeated violations of the rules is punished with dismissal.

SOCIAL PACKAGE

This term refers to extensive social employee benefits. They range from funded stays in sanatoriums and holidays, supplementary health insurance, and university scholarships for the employees' children to greatly subsidised property on the Big Earth, mainly in the southern central regions. Property, for instance in Moscow, St. Petersburg, or in regional capitals, that is sponsored on such a large scale is a promising investment.

TOAST

The phrase: 'To us, to you, to oil and gas!' is a common toast that the people in the oil and natural gas regions like to raise their glasses to. Like many songs, sayings, and poems about the landscape, the abundant resources, the city, or the major companies of the North, this toast is an expression of a special attitude to life. The hard-working people who defy the challenges of the Arctic have actually become fond of the raw material that sustains them. They are aware of the fact that they would not be there without the oil or natural gas.

Quellen
Указание первоисточника
Sources

Sämtliche Zahlen beziehen sich auf Informationen der Pressesprecher von Gazprom in Nowy Urengoi oder wurden den folgenden Quellen entnommen:

Все используемые данные были предоставлены пресс-службой Газпрома в Новом Уренгое либо взяты из приведенных источников:

All figures and statistics were provided by representatives of Gazprom in Novy Urengoy or were taken from the following sources:

www.newurengoy.ru

www.gazprom.com
www.urengoy-dobycha.gazprom.ru
www.yamburg-dobycha.gazprom.ru
www.gazpromexport.ru
www.gazpromquestions.ru

www.novatek.ru
www.wintershall.com

www.ec.europa.eu/Eurostat
www.gks.ru
www.eegas.com
www.entsog.eu

www.oxfordenergy.org

Marlene Laruelle: Russia's Arctic Strategies and the Future of the Far North. M. E. Sharpe, 2014.

Andrei V. Belyi, Andreas Goldthau: Between a rock and a hard place. International market dynamics, domestic politics and Gazprom's strategy. EUI Working Paper RSCAS 2015/22, Robert Schuman Centre for Advanced Studies, 2015.

Florian Stammler, Gertrude Eilmsteiner-Saxinger (Hg.): Biography, Shift-labour and Socialisation in a Northern Industrial City – The Far North: Particularities of Labour and Human Socialisation. Proceedings of the International Conference in Novy Urengoy, Russia, December 2008, Arctic Centre, Rovaniemi.

Roland Götz: Mythen und Fakten. Europas Gasabhängigkeit von Russland. In: Osteuropa, Jg. 62 (6–8/2012), S. 435–458.

David G. Victor (Hg.): Natural gas and geopolitics – from 1970 to 2040. Cambridge University Press, 2006.

Ralf Dickel, Elham Hassanzadeh (et. al.): Reducing European Dependence on Russian Gas – distinguishing natural gas security from geopolitics. OIES Research Paper: NG 92, Oxford Institute for Energy Studies, October 2014.

Biografien
Биографии
Biographies

Die Reise nach Nowy Urengoi, auf die westsibirischen Gasfelder, unternahmen Sophie Panzer und Suzanne Bontemps im Februar 2014. Das Interview mit Wladimir Tamplon führten Sophie Panzer und Christina Simmel im Juli 2015.

Софи Панцер и Сюзанна Бонтемпс отправились в путешествие в Новый Уренгой на западно-сибирские газовые месторождения в феврале 2014 года. Интервью с Владимиром Тамплоном записано Софи Панцер и Кристиной Зиммель в июле 2015 года.

The trip to Novy Urengoy, to the Western Siberian gas fields, was taken by Sophie Panzer and Suzanne Bontemps in February 2014. The interview with Vladimir Tamplon was conducted by Sophie Panzer and Christina Simmel in July 2015.

SUZANNE BONTEMPS

schrieb in den 1980er Jahren als freiberufliche Journalistin Berichte und Reportagen aus der Sowjetunion bzw. Russland unter anderem für das Nachrichtenmagazin „Der Spiegel". Seit Ende der 90er Jahre erarbeitet sie Features für den Hörfunk, meist über gesellschaftspolitische Fragen in Russland. Studium Slawistik und Germanistik in Heidelberg, München und Hamburg.

SOPHIE PANZER

Mitarbeit als Architektin in Büros in Rotterdam, London und Wien. In eigenen Studien und Projekten beschäftigt sie sich mit der Transformation von Städten im postsowjetischen Russland und schreibt als freie Autorin Radiobeiträge über gesellschaftspolitische Themen in Osteuropa. Sie studierte Architektur an der Technischen Universität Delft und East European Studies an der Freien Universität Berlin.

CHRISTINA SIMMEL

studierte Architektur an der Technischen Universität Wien und arbeitet freiberuflich als Architektin und Redakteurin. In der Planung liegt ihr Fokus auf städtebaulichen Studien und Wohnbauprojekten, in einer wissenschaftlichen, theoretischen Auseinandersetzung erforscht sie Prozesse der Urbanisierung und beschäftigt sich mit dem Thema der sozialen Produktion von Räumen.

GERTRUDE SAXINGER

Kultur- und Sozialanthropologin an der Universität Wien und Adjunct Researcher am Yukon College in Whitehorse, Kanada. Ihre Forschungsfelder sind Arbeit und Mobilität (Fly-in/Fly-out/FIFO) in der Bergbau-, Erdöl- und Erdgasindustrie in Kanadas und Russlands Arktis und Subarktis.

СЮЗАННА БОНТЕМПС

Работала в 1980-х годах в качестве независимой журналистки в некоторых изданиях, включая «Шпигель». Делала репортажи из бывшего СССР и России. С конца 90-х работает над репортажами для радио в основном на российские социально-политические темы. Изучала славистику и германистику в Гейдельберге, Мюнхене и Гамбурге.

СОФИ ПАНЦЕР

Как архитектор сотрудничала с бюро в Роттердаме, Лондоне и Вене. Вела собственные проекты и исследования на тему трансформации городской среды в постсоветской России, а также является автором радиорепортажей на социально-политические темы Восточной Европы. Изучала архитектуру в Техническом Университете Делфт, а также восточноевропейские исследования в Свободном Университете Берлина.

КРИСТИНА ЗИММЕЛЬ

Изучала архитектуру в Техническом Университете Вены и работает внештатным архитектором и редактором. Специализируется на исследования по разработке городской среды и на проектах жилищного строительства. Исследует теоретические и научные аспекты урбанизации городской среды, а также изучает проблемы организации социального пространства.

ГЕРТРУДЕ ЗАКСИНГЕР

Культурный и социальный антрополог в Венском университете, научный эксперт в Юконском колледже г. Уайтхорса, Канада. Область исследований: работа и мобильность (Fly-in/Fly-out/FIFO) в горнодобывающей, нефтяной и газовой промышленности Арктики и Субарктики России и Канады.

SUZANNE BONTEMPS

As a freelance journalist, Suzanne Bontemps wrote features and commentary on the Soviet Union, respectively Russia for i. a. the news magazine 'der Spiegel' in the 1980s. Since the late 1990s, she produces radio features, mostly on socio-political issues in Russia. She read German and Slavonic studies in Heidelberg, Munich, and Hamburg.

SOPHIE PANZER

worked as an architect in firms in Rotterdam, London, and Vienna. In her own research projects, she focuses on the transformation of cities in post-Soviet Russia, and she writes features for radio on socio-political issues in Eastern Europe. She holds an MSc in Architecture from Delft University of Technology and an MA in East European Studies from the Free University of Berlin.

CHRISTINA SIMMEL

studied architecture at the Vienna University of Technology and works as a freelance architect and editor. She has academic and professional experience in a range of fields including urban planning and housing development. Her empirical and theoretical research focuses on processes of urbanisation and on the social production of space.

GERTRUDE SAXINGER

Cultural and social anthropologist at the University of Vienna and Adjunct Researcher at the Yukon College in Whitehorse, Canada. Her fields of research are labour and mobility (Fly-in/Fly-out/FIFO) in the mining, oil, and natural gas industries of Canada's and Russia's Arctic and Subarctic regions.

Impressum
Выходные данные
Imprint

Danke für die Unterstützung!
Благодарим за поддержку!
Many thanks for the support!

Team „EnMoTe"
(Environments, Mobilities, Technologies) am Institut
für Kultur- und Sozialanthropologie, Universität Wien

Коллектив «EnMoTe»
(Environments, Mobilities, Technologies) при Институте
культурной и социальной антропологии Венского
университета

Team 'EnMoTe'
(Environments, Mobilities, Technologies) at the De-
partment of Social and Cultural Anthropology of the
University of Vienna

EUROPA
INTEGRATION
ÄUSSERES
BUNDESMINISTERIUM
REPUBLIK ÖSTERREICH

BUNDESKANZLERAMT ▪ ÖSTERREICH

HERAUSGEGEBEN VON
Sophie Panzer, Christina Simmel

AUTORINNEN
Suzanne Bontemps, Sophie Panzer, Christina Simmel

GLOSSAR
Gertrude Saxinger

ÜBERSETZUNG
Deutsch-Russisch: Tatiana Gritsenko, Jörg Alpers
Deutsch-Englisch: Ulf Panzer

LEKTORAT
Deutsch: Johannes Schlebrügge
Englisch: Sarah Gehrke
Russisch: Zoia Novikova

GESTALTUNG, KARTOGRAFIE UND FOTOS
Christina Simmel, Sophie Panzer

LITHOGRAFIE
Pixelstorm Litho & Digital Imaging (Wien)

DRUCK
REMAprint (Wien)

VERTRIEB
Bugrim (Berlin): Deutschland
John Rule, Art Book Distribution (London): Europa
und weltweit
Art Stock Books/IPG (Chicago): USA, Canada

ISBN 978-3-902833-80-8

SCHLEBRÜGGE.EDITOR
Q21 (MuseumsQuartier Wien)
Museumsplatz 1
1070 Wien
Austria
www.schlebruegge.com

ПОД РЕДАКЦИЕЙ
Софи Панцер, Кристины Зиммель

АВТОРЫ
Сюзанна Бонтам, Софи Панцер, Кристина Зиммель

СЛОВАРЬ ТЕРМИНОВ
Гертруде Заксингер

ПЕРЕВОД
Немецкий-русский: Татьяна Гриценко, Йорг Альперс
Немецкий-английский: Ульф Панцер

КОРРЕКТУРА
Немецкий язык: Йоханес Шлебрюгге
Английский язык: Сара Герке
Русский язык: Зоя Новикова

ДИЗАЙН, КАРТОГРАФИЯ И ФОТОГРАФИИ
Кристина Зиммель, Софи Панцер

ЛИТОГРАФИЯ
Pixelstorm Litho & Digital Imaging (Вена)

© 2015 SCHLEBRÜGGE.EDITOR,
выпускающие редакторы и авторы

ПЕЧАТЬ
REMAprint (Вена)

ПРОДАЖА
Bugrim (Берлин): Германия
John Rule, Art Book Distribution (Лондон): Европа и весь мир
Art Stock Books/IPG (Чикаго): США, Канада

ISBN 978-3-902833-80-8

SCHLEBRÜGGE.EDITOR
Q21 (MuseumsQuartier Wien)
Museumsplatz 1
1070 Wien
Austria
www.schlebruegge.com

EDITED BY
Sophie Panzer, Christina Simmel

AUTHORS
Suzanne Bontemps, Sophie Panzer, Christina Simmel

GLOSSARY
Gertrude Saxinger

TRANSLATION
German-Russian: Tatiana Gritsenko, Jörg Alpers
German-English: Ulf Panzer

COPY-EDITING
German: Johannes Schlebrügge
English: Sarah Gehrke
Russian: Zoia Novikova

GRAPHIC DESIGN, CARTOGRAPHY, PHOTOGRAPHIES
Christina Simmel, Sophie Panzer

LITHOGRAPHY
Pixelstorm Litho & Digital Imaging (Vienna)

© 2015 SCHLEBRÜGGE.EDITOR,
editors and authors

PRINTED BY
REMAprint (Vienna)

DISTRIBUTION
Bugrim (Berlin): Germany
John Rule, Art Book Distribution (London): Europe and worldwide
Art Stock Books/IPG (Chicago): USA, Canada

ISBN 978-3-902833-80-8

SCHLEBRÜGGE.EDITOR
Q21 (MuseumsQuartier Wien)
Museumsplatz 1
1070 Wien
Austria
www.schlebruegge.com